THE SPIRIT OF EGYPT
IN AMERICA

By
MICHAEL HINDS
&
TONY CASTRILLI

Edited and cover design by Shadrock
Photography by Shadrock and Richard A Luke.

A Fifth Ribb Publishing Ltd. Production.
ISBN 0-9694907-5-5

FIRST EDITION

No part of this book may be used, copied, printed or broadcast in whole or in part without the consent in writing from the Publishers.

Cover design: Shadrock

All Rights Reserved
Copyright © 1995
by
Fifth Ribb Publishing
P.O. Box 287, Staiton E.
Toronto, Ontario, M6H 4E2
Canada

ISBN 0-9694907-5-5
Printed in Canada

Index

Page No.

Foreword..6

Unmasking the Ku Klux Klan............................26

The Great Whore..38

The Obelisk...51

A Nation of Turmoil....................................56

The Curse of Slavery...................................67

Christmas and the Slave................................72

What Should the Children be Called?....................75

Judaism A Word Created.................................90

The Final Curtain......................................98

The Mountain and the Pit..............................119

The Tree in Egypt.....................................134

<u>WARNING</u>

**This is not an ordinary book for conventional reading.
The contents of this book are extremely sensitive.**

The facts that are written in this book were carefully researched from other books that were written before. Books that were banned, out-of-print, old and new; including the King James version of the Holy Bible, that may soon be out of print.
More and more the King James Bible is becoming a thorn in the side of the system; because of the light of truth it shines in the darkness; contradicting the ways of Christianity.
Other versions are now urgently needed to cover up the truth, and the description of the real children of Israel. Most Christian institutions are now refusing to use the King James Bible.
The contents of this book, might have been written before, but never together in one book. The contents were always written in separate books, for personal or political purpose and ambitions; but never with the Blackman in mind, **except now, and in one book.**
This is the first book that is addressing a subject matter of this nature as a negative for the Blackman.

Please do not read any further
if you are a devout and emotional Christian or Muslim. We do not seek your hurt. Our intentions are crystal clear. We only produce the facts.

This book contains the spiritual answers and revelations that if seen and adhered to by the people of the book (The children of slavery), can cause the downfall of this system; which is not prepared to allow such to happen. Hence spiritual warfare.
Therefore be fore-warned.

There will be a heavy price to pay, when Israelites decide to take back their directional manual (Bible) from the hands of the impostors, heathens, and Gentiles; who have polluted and defiled the words of God.
The sensitive facts about the physical and spiritual destruction of the children of slavery can only be seen with the spiritual eye, even though it is staring us in the face in everyway, everyday.

In this book you will discover the clarity of the prophecy of Deuteronomy the 15th: and the 28th. chapter.
You will notice the similarity between the prophecy of these chapters and the problems facing the children of slavery today.
This subject matter was never written before in the context of black literature.

This book will hurt a lot of people, get a lot of people mad, but I hope it will also strengthen others.

Please take careful attention as you turn the restricted areas of the following pages. Good Luck !

Shadrock

FOREWORD

This book is unlike any other book that has been written on this subject, and so I therefore advise that you do not flip the pages, but rather sit down and read every line very carefully; if you did not grasp the contents, please read it all over again until you understand.

After the writing of the first three books through Fifth Ribb Publishing, it is amazing to find that there is still so much lack of understanding as to why the children of slavery are the way they are. In the other books I tried to show the problems effecting the children of slavery through the scriptures; trying to reveal unto them the walls that needed to be broken down; trying to show the hypocrisy of all the so-called religions in this world. Even if this people read with their own eyes they still find it difficult to understand. I can even say that it is difficult for some to believe.

It is so sad what the Great Whore is doing to a people born to be a chosen of God. A people that is still seeking political and physical solutions to their many unknown spiritual problems. It is sad for those of us who know, and cannot do anything about it, except put words and statements within the pages of a book hoping that the few with leadership ability and intelligence, will guide their community into understanding the spiritual aspect of their lives, which controls every other part of their lives. But I find that even those so-called leaders are themselves ignorant of the spiritual disease(s) implanted in their daily lives. They too are looking for solutions to their own personal problems with the almighty dollar, by seeking through the establishment how they too, like the whiteman, can obtain more and more, but for themselves. There is nothing wrong with a person making money, but when they become obsessed with just making money, the people's problems are forgotten and ultimately become worse. This is a normal way of life for the leadership of the children of slavery, the corrupt shepherds and false prophets are in abundance among us. You only hear their cries when the establishment brings them to their knees, money and all; that is when they call for our support. That is when they too discover that in the eyes of the system they are just another "nigger."

The Nation Of The Lost Tribes Of The House Of Israel through Fifth Ribb Publishing will continue to bring you information on the solution, and hope there would not be a repeat of Sodom and Gomorrah. If we can have ten of every hundred that read Fifth Ribb books, then the God of our fathers might save us, maybe even five; but who am I kidding? It would be a fat chance to find one. And this is a scary fact.

I have shown you in the past, the follies of our spiritual footsteps. I have shown you why you should not drink wine in your place of worship. I have shown you how to pray the way our fathers did before us. I have proven to you that you are indeed the children of the book (the children of Israel). I have introduced you to the light of the doctrine of Israel, shining through the darkness of today's philosophies. I did expose the Christian institution as the Great Whore. I have proven to you that there is no difference between one Christian philosophy from another; from the Catholic to the Evangelist. They are all related by their lies of the cross and the sun. I have shown you the darkness and the burden of the cross, and the evil it brings upon this holy people. Now I am appealing to your good judgment to pay even more attention to what is to be revealed in this book. The following is to be taken very seriously and analysed very carefully.

The KKK and Freemasonry are in full control of the Christian institution, overshadowed by the use of the word "god", on the lips of those in control, followed by their subordinates. The conflict appears among them when the young and ignorant white supremist groups bring their ideology into the open. Then the people with the real power at the top, with the knowledge of control, allow us to believe that they are against racism, while they silently and spiritually practice it.

To the Israelites, the word "god" is good enough. But in the days of Egypt followed by Greece and Rome the word "god" was also used. You must understand that if they worship the sun or the moon, or the image of death, or a snake or beast, to them that is god, so when someone utters the word god, it should not be enough; you must find out first who or what is called god before you make the worst mistake in your life. The term god, or as some pagans might even say "almighty god", is one of the greatest deceptions that the writer will unravel.

To be a member of the Ku Klux Klan you must be a white Christian. To be a member of Freemasonry you must also be a white Christian. Sorry, now anyone can join, but no Israelite can get to the top of this stolen Egyptian way of worshipping the gods (Familiar Spirits, Spirits of Divination) not even close. The KKK is a secret order and so is Freemasonry.

Though today the once secret order known only to the white elite, is now claiming to be open for all to see. Why? Because the eyes of the children of slavery are made blind; they can no longer see spiritual things; if they are shown the evil, they cannot see it; if I, in turn, show them the truth, they cannot see it either. So the ability to choose is lost. Awareness is the first stage of remedy, and if one is not aware of their sickness, then one will never seek the cure. This is the state of affairs that the children of slavery are in today; blind and deaf with the most severe spiritual sickness.

Look at this example very carefully. Albert Pike was a General in the US army, a leader of the KKK, a devout Christian, Chief Judicial Officer, and a Pontifex Maximus of all Freemasonry. General Albert Pike wrote the Bible for the Klan, in which the teachings of Freemasonry were made public. He admitted that to the whiteman Lucifer is the supreme god of LIGHT, WHITE and DIVINE; (Morals and Dogma).

Let us take a closer look at how you may join the Masons, or be a member of the Lodge, and I am not talking about those little lodges that black men and "women" wearing black suits call theirs. No! Those are only there because of the zeal to copy from the whiteman.

I am referring to the real freemasonry, those that have moulded this system and the powerful white administration that controls both church and state.

First you must ask someone who is also a member. In the old days you had to ask three times, then you would be given a petition; then two Masons would have to approve and sign your petition; then it must be taken to the general membership for a vote and such vote must be unanimous in your favour. Still no secret? Today Freemasonry talks more about god than the so-called Christian institutions, yet they claim not to be religious. Another angle to examine is the membership. Today Israelites can join, but one must see how high they can climb socially within the ranks. Most will die and not past the third degree; yet there are thirty three degrees and these are the offices above the third.

The following are the scales. 4th Degree---Secret Master. 5th---Perfect Master. 6th---Intimate Secretary. 7th.---Provost Judge. 8th.---Intendant of the Building. 9th.---Elu of the nine. 10th.---Elu of the Fifteen. 11th.---Elu of the Twelve. 12th.---Master Architect. 13th.---Royal Arch of Solomon. 14th.---Perfect Elu. 15th.---Knight of the East or Sword. 16th.---Prince of Jerusalem. 17th.---Knight of the East and West. 18th.---Knight Rose Croix. 19th.---**Grand Pontiff**. 20th.---Master of the Symbolic Lodge. 21st.---Noachite or Prussian Knight. 22nd.---Knight of the Royal Axe. 23rd.---Chief of the Tabernacle. 24th.---Prince of the Tabernacle. 25th.---Knight of **the Brazen Serpent**. 26th.---Prince of Mercy. 27th.---Knight Commander of the Temple. 28th.--**Knight of the Sun**. 29th.---Knight of St. Andrew. 30th.---Knight Kadosh. 31st.---Inspector Inquisitor. 32nd.---**Master of the Royal Secret**. The 33rd degree is the Grand Commander or Supreme Council.

The symbol for the last three is what is known today as the IRON CROSS, an Egyptian symbol of might and power that was even used by Hitler's Germany, which openly hated black people.These symbols are seen everywhere as symbols of Freemasonry. The beasts are:- Eagles, Horses and Lions etc. Objects are: the Pyramids, Triangles, and the standing stone (Obelisk). Let us not forget the Cross and the Sun.

We must also realize that Freemasonry was taken from the Egyptian philosophy bearing the same strong beasts, Triangles, Serpents, and the symbol of the Sun on top of the obelisks, (standing stones or erected penis). If we look again at the construction of the Christian church-buildings, we will find the cross, the pyramids, and the symbol of the sun. Those who have eyes to see let them see.

To enter into a Ceremonial Temple in the Washington area, you must first past two spiritual guards at the doorway. Two large painted Eggs, or what appear to be such; another symbol of paganism. The practice of colouring eggs, the symbol of the pagan gods of fertility was taken from Egypt, this famous goddess was called Eastre. This so-called goddess is also worshipped by Christians, as the goddess of Spring - Easter. The word god is also mentioned here to deceive. It was from this background that Mr. Pike wrote the bible for the KKK.

Freemasonry itself boasts of being the oldest pagan practice which was copied from the Egyptian BOOK OF THE DEAD.
The very American dollar that makes men mighty has the pyramid surmounted by what they call the all-seeing Eye of God, with Latin phrases above and below. At the base of the Egyptian Pyramid, in Roman numerals is 1776, over the

Pyramids is "Annuit Coeptis", which means according to the authority, "God has favoured our undertaking." The words "Novus Ordo Seclorum" below reads "New Order of the Age" or otherwise **"New Age."** The most important deception continues to be the word "God" - "IN GOD WE TRUST." How can the true and living God that brought His children out of the land of Egypt with a strong right arm, declaring the Egyptians as enemies, be placed in the midst of Egypt today? This is very confusing to me.

On June 20, 1782 the Egyptian Pyramid and the Eye designed by Charles Thomson was approved by the U.S. government to be used as its official seal. This seal or symbol is also used by the Freemasons. If you look carefully you will notice how the practice of Freemasonry and paganism, the culture of Egypt are cleverly integrated into this so-called Christian society.

Let us name a few very important men who were Christians and Masons and at the same time pillars of this great and mighty Egypt, who killed in the name of Lucifer, **their divine god.** They were called fathers of this great nation, who were guilty of the enslavement of our fore parents.

Did you know that thirteen Masons who were also Christians signed the American Constitution on September 17, 1787? Among them were George Washington, the first Master of the ALEXANDRIA-WASHINGTON LODGE No.22; Benjamin Franklin, Grand Master in Pennsylvania; Gunning Bedford Jr., First Grand Master in Delaware; John Blair, First Grand Master in Virginia; and David Brearley, First Grand Master in

New Jersey. We must pay careful attention to what we are noticing. These are men who controlled the very soul of America.

Allow me to go back even a little further, and explained what happened on the Mayflower, the historical vessel that brought these **so-called fathers** to the shores of America (Matthew 23:9). The following was among documents signed in the cabin of this ship. "In the name of God, Amen... Having undertaken for the glory of God, and **the advancement of THE CHRISTIAN FAITH...**"

These were the opening words of the very first State paper. We as Israelites should not be blinded by the use of the word or by the term "god." What is important to note is the fact that they swore to upkeep and advance the Christian faith, whether God is there or not. In the Declaration of Independence, we read, "Appealing to the supreme Judge of the world for the rectitude of our intentions...with a firm reliance on the protection of **divine Providence**."

It was the KKK who judged, sentenced, and hanged us, using the same cross to do so. The Masons who controlled and ruled over us, and the Christians who taught and cleverly turned us into pagans ourselves. We must take this time to stop, think, and come to a logical conclusion that would guide us and our children out of Egypt and out of this spiritual wilderness.

With all that had been quoted above, there is still much more that was hidden, that is hidden, that appears to be hidden, but is really not hidden. Those who have eyes let them see. The word divine means familiar spirits, or spirit of divination, and not of the Almighty God. For the complete breakdown and meaning of the phrase or the word divine see *"The Word The Israelites And The Damned" by yours truly ; from page 122.*

My experience in Washington DC, the murder capitol of the United States, is very frightening to see. Israelites are like zombies (familiar spirits) walking around dead. There is also in this city more than any that I have visited where Egypt is on the lips of every black youth. They are proud to adopt this evil and cursed land as their own for the need of identity. While some black educators and politicians are busy scoring points on the issue of colour, Massa is tightening the economic squeeze, and at the same time exercising his power.
We are failing to see that we are the sacrifice for his wealth and power. Our blood must be shed for his advancement. This is a spiritual fact that we fail to understand.

The greatest industry in America is poverty; our poverty. In the not too distant future thousands of jobs will be created by the government. They will be hiring more law enforcement officers and building more prisons. Israelites make up twelve percent of the general population in the United States, but the latest information received in 1994 is shockingly disgraceful. I have recently learnt that Israelites now make up forty six percent of the prison population.
Let us ask ourselves who do you think is really providing these jobs? Which people are the sacrifice for others to create or even find these jobs? On whose backs are the burdens carried? Israelites in general; the Israelite male in particular.
With the spiritual eye one can see Egypt all over again. What is also obvious is that most of the images of the beasts and marks of power were given to the United States by Rome, another

destroyer of God's people (the Israelites). One such monument is even called by the name SACRIFICE; a gift from the people of Italy, to the people of the United States of America. Yet these Israelites are either turning to these same gods for help, not realizing that they are the sacrificial lambs to these strange gods which our forefathers have not known.

Everytime we celebrate Easter, know that it is pagan. Everytime we involve our children with Halloween; it is an abomination. To celebrate the time of the dead (October 31 - November 2) is totally wrong. God said that He is not a God of the dead. (Matthew 22:32). One of the greatest deceptions of all is Christmas. (December. 21-25) This is also a pagan festival of sacrifice to the gods, and from the 26th to the first of January is yet another feast and sacrifice to the two-faced god called Janus. Yet black people are calling it their black Christmas, or the time of Harvest. What fruit can be harvested at this time of year? We are just being ridiculously stupid copy-cats.

Everytime we join the heathen to celebrate thanksgiving, we break the law of God. We are not suppose to keep a feast to any other god, and if we must keep a feast, or celebrate, how come we are forgetting the EXODUS? (Exodus 12:1-2) Whatever happened to Passover? Oh I forgot; according to Christianity, it is gone with Jesus. Another lie to trap our minds into celebrating a false feast to a false god.

Shouldn't this most miraculous event be remembered by the children of the most High God? How come this is forgotten by the children of slavery? Everywhere in the holy scriptures it is

mentioned. The heathens are giving thanks to their gods for their land, for their slaves and their wealth. What are you giving thanks for anyway? For poverty, sickness, or homelessness?
Do not believe for one minute that their wealth is of God. If you do, you might as well believe also that Babylon, Egypt, Greece, and Rome received their wealth and power from God for they too were mighty nations. It is said in the book of (Matthew 4: 8-9), that Satan would have given Jesus the wealth and power of this world if he should bow down and worship him. For those of you who do not read the new testament; remember at one time all countries depended on Egypt, the way they are depending on America today (Genesis 41:57).

What we are experiencing today is a similarity of what happened when our fathers went into Canaan. The only difference is, that our fathers knew then that the gods were false, while today we are deceived into believing that all paths lead to the same god. This is a vicious lie! Our forefathers and mothers were supposed to destroy the Canaanites and break down and destroy their altars with the images and idols (Exodus 23:20-25), but the images were so beautiful, in contrast with their God who they could not see, that they felt compassion for the idols, and worshipped them and suffered at the hands of our God.
The Bible says in Psalms 115: 4-9 and 135: 15-18 " The idols of the heathen are silver and gold the work of men's hands. They have mouths but they speak not, eyes have they but they see not. They have ears, but they hear not, neither is there any breath in their mouths. They that make them are like unto them, so is everyone that trusteth in them". Therefore I say unto you seek you first the cause of the sickness, then find the cure in the Laws, statutes and commandment of The God of our Fathers..

To enter into Washington DC, there is the symbol of the beast, four lions. Two when you are entering, and two when you are leaving. There are also the signs of the Pyramids in their architecture; the symbol of the serpent on their monuments and their institutions; the symbol of the sun (a small globe) or the cross, or just a plain circle on top of the obelisks on their churches. How can we as a people progress in this world of evil, if we do not understand the difference between good and evil, clean and unclean, God and Lucifer, life and death ?
Since the Christian churches have out grown the neighbourhood cemeteries, they still allow the cemetery to remain inside and on top of their buildings. (Matthew 23; 27) "Woe unto you Scribes and Pharisees, hypocrites! for ye are like unto whited sepulchres, which indeed appear beautiful outward, but are within full of dead men's bones, and of all uncleanness."

Because the enemy has us talking colour, we are missing and not seeing the real danger in living and acting like Egyptians ourselves.
 Even the "X" that we wear on our caps, and our clothes, is in the shape of the very cross that killed Andrew a disciple of the Christ, who was nailed upside down on one. We wear it proudly as black people in ignorance.
This too is part of our destructive symbol (Colossians 2:14). According to the scriptures, the cross is contrary to us because of the burden nailed to it. See *"The Truth The Lie And The Bible" by yours truly; from page 64.* Even the evil earrings that our men wear in their ears are the jewels to identify an Egyptian or Ishmaelite; (Judges 8:24).
Let us now look at the obelisks. Why in God's name did the Christian so-called church remove the obelisks from Egypt?

Why not build their own type of monument? History tells us that they did try, but not to build their own type, they just copied and built another obelisk, "The Washington Monument," and what happened? It was seized, the battle was raging, a minister had to travel to Italy to learn what the Italians had learnt about the Pyramids and Obelisks of Egypt. BLOOD HAD TO BE SPILLED.

The cornerstone was laid July 4, 1848. The construction work carried it to 152 feet in 1853. For years no work was done or could have been done. This was the period when Israelites were being slaughtered in the south. The civil war also started in this period. Take note of the confusion. Is this not a spiritual thing? Then in 1884 a 3300 pound marble capstone with a pyramid was placed at the top of this Obelisks which now stands 555 feet, 5 1/8 inches tall.
Think of all the spiritual happenings and sacrifices that occurred in the building of this Monument.

Why would the so-called Christian Powers spend so much time and money to remove the Original Egyptian Pagan gods and place them on their seat of power? Why place even the imitation on top of their own godly Christian church buildings; along with the sign of the Pyramids? Why use the sign of the Egyptian, later the Greek god of Medicine, the Serpent coiling around the cross in hospitals and ambulances? Why? Why would a so-called Christian church teach the story of how God cursed the Egyptians written in the books of Moses, and at the same time associate themselves with Egypt? You still do not understand? Then let the blind lead the blind, and the dead bury the dead. Those who have eyes to see, let them see.

The enemy knows that we only look at the skin colour. He involves us on this issue daily by stirring up dirt based on skin-colour so as to keep us all occupied with the less serious matter. He gradually unfolds his plans with ease, taking his own time in doing so, knowing full well that the Israelites and their leadership are too busy talking colour to notice the real root cause of their problems.

The Egyptians enslaved our fathers before, because we broke the most important commandment of all; **"Hear Oh Israel The Lord our God is one Lord."** Mark 12:29, "And Jesus answered him, the first of all the commandments is Hear O Israel the Lord our God is one Lord." Yet we cannot understand, to serve another is a deadly sin; and we are doing the same thing today, by serving a divine god that does not know us, and ignoring our own God.

When we take a careful look at the full picture, we notice among the many activities of Lucifer one very familiar one that keeps repeating itself, and that is to give life. When he was in the garden of God (Ezekiel 28: 13) he knew almost everything except how to administer the breath of life. Now he through the gentiles, his fallen angels, and agents are trying desperately to do it, if we look around and see the computer games, the robots, the talking dolls, and walking toys and we find it amazing, but what is hidden is really not seen. A relentless effort; but if one is of the dead he will always be of the dead, for the day that man is able to manufacture blood and produce flesh and bones, Lucifer has won, but they can't. Thank God! For the scriptures states that God will capture death His last enemy. This proves one thing, that the man Lucifer is no wimp as the Christian philosophy constantly wants us to believe. These very Christians are part of the machinery of death that will also be destroyed. I Corinthians 15: 26, "The last enemy that shall be destroyed is death".

Now I am taking this opportunity to introduce to you a deeper message. A spiritual revelation. A new way of exposing the secrets that are really no secrets; hoping that you might be able to put the pieces together, to lift the spiritual burden off your shoulders once and for all through other messengers. Other names among the flock of my brethren. God has also blessed them with the spirit of understanding to enable them to understand the doctrine, and to see beyond the colour of their skin. In this book we shall go below the surface

First let me introduce you to my brothers **Michael Hinds and Tony Castrilli;** Michael is the assistant Chief Priest in The House Of Israel (Canada), now living in Atlanta Georgia, Tony is a teaching Priest and the scribe. Michael is also the investigative researcher and former editor of the Israelite Chronicle. Michael is inquisitive, he's curious. He provides yet another thorn of truth in the system. How do you describe a man that is quiet as the grass, knowledgeable as the past, confident as the roar of thunder? He seeks, he searches, and he plunders into the mysteries of darkness and light, good and evil, top to bottom, success and failures. He asks, why are things the way they are? What can be done to make things better for my people? Why the tears? Why the pain? Why is the cross so heavy upon the shoulders of my people? Why the curse of the God of my fathers surrounds them like a stumbling stone? Why?

He has within him the three "tions" of dynamism that make an excellent Israelite investigator. Determina**tion**, Dedica**tion**, and as you turn the pages of this book you will recognize his valuable Contribu**tion**.
On the other hand, Tony as the co-Author is very knowledgeable in the area of science based on Biblical facts, as you will notice in his articles: "The Mountain and the Pit, and The Tree In Egypt"

They dig beneath the depths of the past, fan the flames of the present, and reaches beyond the heights of the future. They are men who are completely moved by the faith of their belief. Completely strong in the works of their God, and sincerely hopeful for this people, and this makes me very proud of them. The pages of this book reveals the length that they both will go to get to the bottom of not only the cause of the problem, but also provide a taste of the solution.
Before you turn the pages of their writings, be prepared to be your own person, by this I mean you must be able to see things as they are. Pray for the greatest gifts of all; Knowledge, Wisdom and Understanding. Remember the Spirit of understanding is never given to fools.

Before I go let me make my last comment. **They say that America is the land of the free and home of the brave; but I say America is the LAND of the gods and HOME of the Slaves.**
Revelation 18:4 reads, "And I heard another voice from heaven saying come out of her my people that ye be not partakers of her sins, and that ye receive not of her plagues." We must get out now before it is too late; after all we are not Christians, neither are we Muslims. We should stop worshipping WOOD

AND STONE. The children of slavery are indeed the children of Israel, and from henceforth we must be proud to let the world know that we are the people of the book, ISRAELITES. We cannot remove ourselves physically from this Egypt, because it is said in the book of Deuteronomy the twenty eight chapter, verse sixty eight: "We shall see it (land of Israel) no more again". We can be in America, but not of America. We therefore must separate ourselves from her philosophies. We must be able to teach the rest of America about the true and living **God of Israel.**

This must be the first stage of consciousness, and the first state of awareness, that we should come to, before we start our spiritual journey. We should stop taking so much of our valuable time to discuss "colour", when we should in fact be discussing righteous Power; Spiritual and Physical.

We must bear one thing in mind. No one can really go within themselves. This statement used so regularly by people who practice Yoga or those who claim to be Buddhist is also a spiritual error made by Israelites. Without the knowledge of truth, this practice will appear attractive, but is rather very dangerous. When one empties him or herself in a state of what is known today as meditation, all that is simply happening, is you are deliberately suppressing or dismissing your own spirit for the taking over or the occupation of your body by another entity or spirit, which will then control your being. Without the knowledge of truth, think what can happen to you when you provide a home for the dead in your own body, and when you encourage without knowledge evil spirits that are always around us.

With truth you will be made aware of the spiritual transformation of self, and learn and pray how to strengthen your own spirit for your own spiritual strength, rather than travel in the restricted areas and danger zones of your spirituality. Allowing some person(s) who is already dead, (familiar spirit) to be using your body for the glorification of their own lost soul.

This warning is for everyone in general but for Israelites in particular. Without the oneness, and the single accord of this people, physically, and spiritually, we are doomed for destruction. We must remember there is no S in sheep to describe the quantity. Whether we are one or one million we should spiritually be in one accord, serving one God, under one law. After all we are the sheep of His pasture (Psalms 79: 13. Jeremiah 23:1). We are Israelites!

As you turn the following pages you will discover why people like Michael Jackson, and O.J. Simpson are making such an impact on the entire world in their darkest days. You will discover the root cause of our dilemma. The root cause of our sickness. The root cause of our many diseases. The root cause of our poverty; the root cause of our social behaviour. The root cause of all of our problems, also the root cause of our ignorance. You will also discover that we had been brought into Egypt again with ships as bondmen and bondwomen. Read Deut. 28: especially from verses 54-68. You will discover

THE SPIRIT OF EGYPT IS IN AMERICA.

May your eyes be opened and may the God of our fathers - The God Of Abraham, The God Of Isaac and The God Of Jacob bless you and yours real good.

ABOUT THE PHOTOGRAPHS

The photographs in this book, will help to explain the deception of this Christian system. They will show the parallel between paganism and Christianity.

You will notice the symbol of the sun; the tree; the serpent; the the hewned stone; the cross and the dead. The natural eye had seen all these and more before, but the lack of knowledge kept us from understanding.

Taking a look at the evil of **the hewn stone or erected penis, and the vagina hidden in the deception of a clever painting**.

These symbols appearing together will resurrect the real sexual custom of ancient Egypt in the worshipping of the sun-god Ra(Isis & Osiris). The Obelisk itself is also in defiance of the Living God, and contrary to His instructions. Exodus 20:25 "And if thou shall make me an altar of stone, thou shalt not build it of hewn stone, for if thou lift up thy tool upon it; thou hast polluted it".

Knowing that this was the altar of the Egyptians, why would this Christian society honour it, or even use it, or have it on their soil?

You will notice **the symbol of the sun** being worshipped all over again.

Ezekiel 8:16-17 "And he brought me into the inner court of the Lord's house; and behold at the door of the temple of the Lord, between the porch and the altar were about five and twenty men with their backs toward the temple of the Lord and their faces toward the east; and **they worshipped the sun** towards the east. Then he said unto me, hast thou seen this O son of man? Is it a light thing to the house of Judah **that they commit the abominations** which they commit here?..."

You will notice the prominence of **the Fir, evergreen, or Christmas tree** which is the symbol of Lucifer always by their place of worship, or in the cemetery. This tree as described in the book of Ezekiel fits the description perfectly as the true representation of Lucifer. Note that it is unlike any tree, it is evergreen throughout all the seasons of the year, and it is also worshipped during the pagan feasts from Dec. 21st.-25th. It is a Fir tree similar to the one mentioned in the Bible. Ezekiel 31.

The symbol or rather the **image of the serpent** is on almost every aspect of modern life; e.g. Hospitals, Libraries, Memorial Monuments, etc. This is not to be confused with the serpent that Moses made as some will try to say. This is the serpent that was in the garden, that was cursed by God. The book of Isaiah explains. Isaiah 27:1 "In that day the Lord with his sore and great, and strong sword shall punish Leviathan the piercing serpent, even Leviathan that crooked serpent and he shall slay the dragon that is in the sea".

The other evil is really the ultimate objective of all God's enemy; **the worshipping of the dead;** since He is the God of the living, what better way to go against him, but to raise up the status of the dead, by praying to them, praying for them, and praying with them. Psalms 106: 28 "They joined themselves also unto Baalpeor and ate the sacrifices of the dead." Such was the abomination and the evils of men. Now take a very close look at Christianity and their divine god.

SHADROCK

UNMASKING THE KU KLUX KLAN

"What appears to be is not, but what is not, is!" Confusing?! This helps to stimulate and prepare the mind for what is ahead. Simplified, it means that some things are not always what they appear to be, since the true identity is usually hidden. In this article, where most people see men, we shall see snakes and fiery serpents at that, which do not even belong in this physical world. But which, after choosing to crawl on their bellies, rather than practise the truth, have returned to seduce others into their lifestyle, hissing to each other in secret. In their corner of darkness and death, we shall shine the light of Truth and offer the water of Life.

In a world dominated by the spirit of deception, we Israelites must be extremely vigilant regarding our daily activities. The manifestations of deception will occur more frequently as the biblical prophecies unfold. We must not be dismayed, but rather seek the hidden agenda and focus on our responsibilities. A prime example of this deception is the KU KLUX KLAN. This Christian pagan cult is fundamentally old fashioned fire-worship renewed. Its masonic foundation dictates an atmosphere of tension and conflict. Its "racist" platform, or more accurately, its **theory** of white supremacy, is just a clever disguise to distract from the real purpose of the organization. In fact, we should get use to looking at the exact opposite scenario first, we may avoid many problems in life. We shall see that the K.K.K pays fervent homage to Nimrod, a Cushite or Ethiopian, a man greatly kissed by the sun, i.e. pure black, like a thousand midnights; and so does Freemasonry and Christianity. The mystery is just that - secrecy.

The symbols of the Klan are: 1) the cross [death]; 2) fire [their interpretation of the sun]; and 3) the serpent [Lucifer]. These will be explained later, but first let us examine the name "Ku Klux Klan." Like most pagan rituals, fire-worship originated in Babylonia with Nimrod. Genesis 10:8-10 talks about this extremely powerful black king. Genesis 11:1-9 details his confrontation with the God of Israel. As the head of the Cyclops, who were called the "kings of the flame", he was called KUCLOPS.

Also in Chaldea, as well as Egypt, a ritual in honour of the dead was performed as part of the sacred mysteries. This death ritual was called the "KUKLOS ANAGKES", or the "Unavoidable Cycle", or simply the "circle of necessity". Here we have the origin of the "innocent" Christian funeral service of bringing their dead to their altar; but that is another article. The original name for the K.K.K. was "the circle". As we learn more about the worship of the sun-god, we shall see how important the circle becomes. A deliberate attempt to flirt with mysticism, just like the "harmless" college fraternity, produced "KUKLOS". Kuklos is the Greek word for circle, hence, "KUKLUX". "KLAN" was added since the six founding young men were of Scottish and Irish descent - Gentiles.

Originally the Klan was founded out of boredom, as a fun thing; but my mother used to say while wagging her fore finger, "the devil always find work for idle hands". Furthermore, God's chosen people, the Israelites, were just freed from physical slavery, so something had to be done about that. We know the prophecy! By way of their dress, the Klan pretended to represent evil spirits from another world, scaring the rural folks at night. The freed slaves, being a very spiritual people, took this matter seriously, showing extreme fear. The Klan's fascination with the dark side of spirituality and the response from the black population, fanned the flames of the K.K.K. This mystical adventure would lead the Klan on a spiritual path of evil, which very few people would really understand. It should be quite evident by now that the Ku Klux Klan is not simply the "racist" organization many have been misled to believe; but rather part of the manifestation of the Great Whore in this world - in their own words, **"an Invisible Empire"**. The Emperor or Spiritual Leader is that old serpent Lucifer. Later we shall see that the K.K.K. cannot function effectively without its other evil associates [Orders] - Christianity and Freemasonry.

In order to understand, we must look for the hidden symbols on which the three Orders thrive - tension, conflict, guilt, fear and ignorance. Of course all this is cleverly masked with words of love, peace and progress, as a cover for the effectiveness of the real purpose. We will clearly see the "Invisible Empire" at work with a distinct system and doctrine, which employs two major branches - one for the initiates [Freemasonry] and one for the masses [Christianity]. Christianity and Freemasonry, as branches of the same tree, are further divided into other groups. The Klan has become one such sub-division and its adoption by masonry is used as an instrument of the Great Whore. After the abolition of slavery, for example, through the use of the Klan, the Great Whore was able to effectively control the Israelites and maintained the status quo of the American South. Needless to say, this treatment of the Israelites had been prophesied in the bible, so there should not be any surprises. The choice was ours then as it is now, the blessing, or the curse. Read **Leviticus chapter 26 and Deuteronomy chapter 28**.

From its social club style origins in 1866 the K.K.K evolved into a full secret masonic-type Order by 1915. Most of the Klan's major leaders were Freemasons and membership was restricted to white American-born Gentile Christians. One very important

Klansman was **Gen. Albert Pike [1809-1891]**, who held the office of Chief Judicial Officer. Pike, the Pontifex Maximus of all Freemasonry, was the author of "Morals and Dogma" or "MAD", which was written in 1871 and has become the "bible" of masonry worldwide. In Freemasonry, Lucifer is seen as the god of light, instead of the god of darkness and evil, and is worshipped as the son of the morning [sun-god]. Unfortunately, only the very few masons at the top of the pyramid understand this important fact. The others are cleverly deceived, which is one of the main functions of the lodge anyway. **The Freemasons know and do teach that Lucifer was not black, unlike the others of the Garden of Eden**, [since he was not created in the image and likeness of God]. The majority of the so-called elite of this world are affiliated with masonry, regardless of political ideology. This helps to explain the "MAD" state of affairs today, since they all follow the script given by Albert Pike, whether directly or indirectly.

In addition to Pike, some of the earliest Freemasons were called the Knights of the Temple of Solomon, (not to be confused with Solomon of the bible) or Knights Templar, the Gentile Christian Order from 1118. Under the patronage of King James VI of Scotland [same as James I of England] masonry flourished from 1590 in Scotland and expanded to England. Most of the Grand Masters of the Grand Lodge of England (1717) were Christian Priests. In fact, freemasonry, as practised today, originated within the Christian Institution. King James himself was a Grand Master - 1567 (Scotland) and 1603 (England); and of course since Henry VIII, the English monarchy automatically heads the Christian Institution in England and eventually the entire British Empire. The Order of the Rosy Cross, or Rosicrucians, is another Christian Order dating back to the late 1500's. In 1776, a Khazarian, Adam Weishaupt, who became a Jesuit Christian

Priest, founded the Order of the Illuminati in Bavaria. This Order also included many Protestant reformers, both Lutherans and Calvinists. The Khazarian role in freemasonry is so intriguing that it must be treated as a separate article.

In pagan Rome, where Christianity originated, fire was worshipped as the great purifier; while the Epidaurian snake was worshipped as the representative of Aesculapius. The pagan, Gentile Greeks claimed that this snake possessed the power to heal, since Aesculapius was their god of medicine. Today, that same snake is wrapped around a cross and displayed on ambulances, or at various medical institutions. On the Christian "Good Friday", their Pope prostrates himself before a cross of fire in worship of Saturn, the Babylonian fire-god. Of course Saturn is just another name for Nimrod. According to pagan historians, in 312 A.D., Constantine is said to have had the vision of a fiery cross and told to use it to conquer. It should be made extremely clear that this vision was not of the God of Truth. **We should also note how effective that fiery cross has been in conquering the spirits of the Elect of God - the Children of Slavery.** So the next time your so-called church choir starts to lament the solemn sounds of "The Old Rugged Cross" you should understand what is really meant. Even Jesus the Christ spoke of the cross as a terrible burden and a destructive instrument. He never said to pay homage to it; in fact it eventually killed him, just as it did many other Israelites.

The Imperial emblem of the Roman Emperor, who was also the Pontifex Maximus or the chief fire- and serpent-worshipper, was a red serpent on a purple background. The Romans encircled the head of the image of Aesculapius with rays, [sun] just like the Christians who encircle the head of the graven image of their god today, whom they call "Jesus". Aesculapius or Phaethon was none other than that great, black Babylonian god, Nimrod, who was worshipped as "the child of the sun". Today, due to the awareness of "racism', the name may change, but the practise is the same. **This makes Sunday worshipping, Freemasonry or Christianity as practised by the devils in disguise, a vicious crime against the laws of God. For the Children of Slavery, it is the greatest possible manifestation of their state of bondage.**

As a secret Christian masonic Order, the K.K.K clearly reflects the dark side of spirituality in its hierarchy and symbols. It is headed by an Imperial Wizard, with his ten Genii; a Grand Dragon, with his eight Hydras; a Grand Titan, with his six Furies; a Grand Giant, with four Goblins; a Grand Cyclops, with two Night Hawks; and Magi. All Klansmen are known officially as "Ghouls" and utilize secret passwords, hand shakes and signals. The emblem or flag of the K.K.K specifically identifies it as an Order of secret fire-worshippers, or disciples of Lucifer. The flag is yellow, shaped like a triangle, and had a scalloped red border to simulate a flame. In the middle is a black Flying Dragon. We should understand that fire-worship and serpent-worship are synonymous. Of course, we are all aware of the fire-breathing dragon, or the fiery serpent of **Revelation chapter 12**. Even the tapered or conical shape of the tall hoods worn by the Klansmen is symbolic of the flame of a lighted candle. The white robes, as a symbol of deception, help to conjure up a ghostly image and thereby enhance their evil spirituality.

Since the time of its inception, the Klan has continued to draw on Christianity for its strength. Originally, most of its members were Methodists and Presbyterians. On October 12, 1921, while testifying before a Congressional Committee, Imperial Wizard Col. William J. Simmons explained that the Klan was a Christian Order. Col. Simmons, a Christian of the Methodist-Episcopal Church, steered the Klan along its evil mystical path, complete with prayers, oaths, hymns and other rituals. Between 1922 and 1925 it was next to impossible to tell the difference between the Christian Fundamentalists and the K.K.K. Approximately 40,000 Fundamentalists joined the Klan, most of them ministers who held high positions within this institution.

Mormon ministers were delighted to join, since Mormonism employed similar secret rites as Masonry and showed the same disdain for the Children of Slavery. The truth is, the more knowledgeable the white, pagan, Gentile Christian became about the history of humanity, the more envious he was of the black man, especially the Israelite. Some 67% of the national speakers used by the Klan were Fundamentalist Christians. **The fact is that Christianity and the Ku Klux Klan are unified by the same symbol of death - the cross.**

Let us try to understand the significance of this malignant instrument, otherwise known as the cross. We must ask ourselves where would we go to find the cross in abundance. The obvious answer should be the cemetery. However, do not be disappointed for thinking of the Christian Establishment, since **the cross, the cemetery and the Christian Institution go together. They all represent DEATH, which along with the serpent are the symbols of Lucifer.** Throughout the old British Empire, the Christian place of worship was strategically located in the middle of the cemetery. The same holds true of the Roman, Spanish, American and other Christian Empires. There was absolutely no access to or from the Christian god without first "paying your respects to the dead". **Now that same cross has been removed from the grave site and placed at the Christian altar. At birth, they brand us with it in our forehead, just like the slave master. At adulthood, we stand before it to qualify for marriage; and at death it is placed at our head. This is the most effective spiritual system every devised - the recycling of the enslaved dead.** It makes no difference whatsoever that the Christian sect, a.k.a the Ku Klux Klan, cares to illuminate their cross for greater spiritual impact, they are all disciples of Lucifer, the god of the dead.

On December 15, 1993 I had the opportunity to view the Imperial Wizard, a.k.a the National Director of the K.K.K, speak on U.S. national television. When asked to explain the "flaming cross", since the hostess of the show was of the opinion that the "good" Christian symbol of the cross should not be desecrated with fire, Mr. Thomas Robb made some rather interesting comments. He confirmed that the flaming cross is a Christian symbol which predates the Klan and is presently used throughout the Christian Establishment, naming several popular denominations which use it is an official capacity. In effect, there was no difference between the Klan and Christianity, the results were the same - enslavement of the Israelites. Mr. Robb further stated that black people should be proud of their heritage and culture. In other words, the culture and heritage of the Children of Slavery does not include Christianity, so they should leave it alone to the Gentile European. How true!

However, the reason that brought the Imperial Wizard to the T.V. studio, was in defence of a Gentile Christian boy who was barred from wearing his Klan's cap to school, while an Israelite boy was permitted to wear his Malcolm X cap. In the opinion of the Imperial Wizard, Malcolm was a "racist" just like the Klan, so he saw no difference in the symbol on both caps. Naturally, the discussion that ensued revolved around the Klan and Malcolm X, in favour of Malcolm, by both black and white. Everybody missed the golden opportunity to observe that Malcolm X, the Ku Klux Klan and Christianity all promoted the same deadly cross. **Whether in the form of a "T" or an "X"; within a circle or attached to a circle; whether it is called the Crux Commissa [Tau] or the Crux Ansata [Ankh], it is still a cross.**

It is simply that old Egyptian and Babylonian symbol of death, used in their pagan Mystery Systems for initiation and worship, that has been adopted by pagan Christianity. What is now identified with Malcolm is called the Crux Decussata or the cross of St. Andrew. It is believed that Andrew, the Israelite disciple of Jesus the Christ, was murdered on a cross in the shape of an "X". It must be stated, especially to the black youths, that many of their Israelite ancestors were murdered on this same cross by the Gentile Romans, with their head downward and their feet upward, forming an "X" with their body. It is the most shameful manner in which any human being may be put to death. This same cross that is nothing but a symbol of the enslaved dead, creating zombies out of the very elect of God, the Israelites. This symbol should be scorned.

Hopefully many people may now see that this matter goes much deeper than just fashion. In fact, only a fool would consider using a cross as a fashion statement, unless, of course, that person is a Christian pagan or a child of Satan. When we hear the name "Hitler", for example, many automatically think of hatred or murder. Yet if we really think about this matter seriously, **our dictionaries could read as follows: - Christianity - Ku Klux Klan, evil, lies, murder, hatred and deception.** Many people do not know that the swastika or gammadion is also a cross, originating among the Egyptians and Chaldeans, then adopted by the Buddhists of India and China. The fact is that there was no difference between the Nagas of Egypt, Chaldea and the Hindu of India. The Nagas were among the highest spiritually educated people on earth, a special Priesthood of black people. I really hate to use the word "black", since everybody was black in that Nile-Tigris-Euphrates-Indus region at the time; but because of this pagan Christian culture in which we now live, it has to be stated. In fact, it is very important because the caste system of the Hindu was not originally based on colour or race, but on occupation; unlike what the so-called Aryans would like to portray. A similar system existed in Egypt and is even being moulded today on a global scale.

The Nagas were serpent-worshippers and believed their first king or ruler to be a serpent. Is it a coincidence that the pre-dynastic [prior to 3500 B.C.] rulers of Egypt were called Nagadah, and every Pharaoh since wore the symbol of the serpent on his crown? Let us not lose sight of the fact that the serpent is also the symbol of the Klan and is on par with the cross; hence the connection between Lucifer, Egypt, Buddha, the Klan, Christianity, and Hitler.

Hitler, who died a Christian, proudly adorned himself with the iron cross or croiz patee [pate, paty], also called the pyramid cross, from which the swastika may have evolved originally. This is the exact same iron cross that is found on the crowns and sceptres of many Gentile Christian monarchs. This same cross is also called the Templar cross, from the Knights Templar and is used before the signature of the Grand Commander in some Masonic Lodges. The Knights Templar were granted the iron cross in 1146, to be used as a crest, by the Christian Pope Eugenius III. In 1934, Hitler made plans to form the Order of the Brotherhood of the Templars, otherwise known as the Schutzstaffel or the "SS", with the iron cross as its symbol. In addition, the swastika, when used with the signature of a Mason, is called the Hermetic cross and represents a member of the governing body of that Order. Plus, many Christian Establishments are not ashamed to display the seal of the OTO [Ordo Templi Orientis] at their place of worship. This Order played a key role in the founding of Hitler's Germany. It is indeed very difficult to tell where Christianity begins and Masonry ends.

Thus Hitler would have been the "messiah" of Christianity, the very embodiment of the K.K.K, Freemasonry and Christianity. Let us never forget that Hitler's Vice Chancellor, Mr. Franz von Papen, was the Vatican's number one man in Germany. Also, in the Supreme Court of the NSDAP, the highest authority in Hitler's Germany, a large crucifix towered above the swastika.

The symbol of the cross within a circle is used by Christianity, Masonry, the K.K.K and others whose philosophical foundation is based on the theory of white supremacy. Have you taken a good look at the symbol of NATO? This should send you scrambling to find Revelation chapters 17 and 18. The Great Whore is so powerful, so evil and so intricately woven within this present civilization, that God Himself must come down and destroy her. Surely many may say that this is nothing but paranoia; but in all fairness many do not really understand what is going on. Let us look at the situation from another angle. Why would the brilliant minds of Christianity name their highest place of worship a basilica, their priests rectors, and the residence of their priests a rectory? Of all the words to choose from, certainly they could have done better.

The fact is that the serpent (basilisk) and homosexuality (**rect**um) go together - Rom. 1:18-32. However, does this mean that because the pagan Gentiles of Judaism use the Star of David, that they are on par with the Israelites? **No**! Matt. 7:15-20 helped to prepare us for this deception - by their fruits we shall know them. Also read Rev. 2:9 and 3:9 which specifies that those calling themselves Jews are liars of the synagogue of Satan. Now compare NATO's response to Bosnia (Yugoslavia) with their response to Iraq, Panama, Grenada, Somalia, Haiti, etc. Therefore, I rest my case; so much for the lies of the Grand Lodge of Christianity and the deception of the knights of the Ku Klux Klan. After all this, how can the Children of Slavery honestly justify their involvement in the institution of Christianity, or Freemasonry?

THE GREAT WHORE

It is common knowledge among people who understand the mysteries of the kingdom of God through His doctrine (understanding being a gift from the God of the Israelites), that this whole world has been deceived by Lucifer, the god of the dead. The greatest manifestation of this deception is found in the culture, philosophy or ideology of the Gentiles, which is commonly known as Christianity. These Gentile heathens, entertaining the spirit of the air, originally settled in the northern lands of Europe or Europa, from whence their pagan culture expanded, to eventually dominate the entire world, seducing other nations like a great whore.

THE FOUNDATION OF THE GREAT WHORE

This Great Whore has in turn manifested herself in three distinct, but secretly united Orders or Establishments. These Establishments or Institutions then branched off into various other groups, ranging from the K.K.K to the Nazis to the skinheads. Individually, there is a very good chance that your local Christian priest, pastor or evangelist is a disciple of the Great Whore. Other whoremongers would include law enforcement agencies, politicians, the legal system, and most businessmen. At the head of the Great Whore is the Order of Khazarism or Judaism; her body forms the Order of Freemasonry; and her legs, the Order of Christianity. Each Order is in turn headed by a secret elite group, which leads it into battle against the other Orders for supremacy. The three Orders secretly engage in much lying, treachery and deceit in preparation for that dreaded day when this Great Whore will be officially wedded to her husband Lucifer and the Anti-Christ will be specifically revealed. All of this in-fighting is played out in the lives of the inhabitants of this world, who are not aware of what is secretly taking place, but most are eagerly caught up in the action, just like pawns in a game of chess.

The trademark of the Great Whore is secrecy (darkness), deceit (lies) and chaos (violence), all of which lead to her fruits of death, which is in turn the source of her strength. This fact may easily be seen when she is stripped of her cloak of secrecy, which can only be done effectively by one possessing the spirit of truth. This gift of truth may only be granted by the God of the Israelites, who is the only God of Truth, according to the scriptures. When an analysis of the fruit of the Great Whore is performed after removing the lid of her deception, only a practising Israelite will see that there is no "Jew" in Judaism; no "freedom" in Freemasonry; and no "Christ" in Christianity. Yet, by imposing a standard of secrecy, the Great Whore created an atmosphere of mystery, which appeals to the curiosity and fantasies of the unfulfilled mind and allows for their easy seduction.

In order to fully understand the Great Whore, one has to reference the Israelite scriptures; but not so much the book of Revelation, as many would want to do, but rather the first book of Genesis. This makes very good sense both physically and spiritually, since the book of Genesis forms both the introduction and foundation of truth, and common sense dictates that one begins at the beginning. In Gen. 2:16-17, God explicitly commands Adam, as the first representative of humanity, regarding what he should or should not do. "**Of every tree of the garden thou mayest freely eat; but of the tree of the knowledge of good and evil, thou shalt not eat of it: for in the day that thou eatest thereof thou shalt surely die.**" As our God speaks, every word becomes law - permanent law, that only He alone can ever repeal. It should be quite evident that the tree of the knowledge of good and evil is Lucifer; but those who require further proof may want to read the book of Ezekiel, chapt. 28, especially verses 11-19. Then read chapt. 31 in order to put it all together. To eat of this tree then, this tree of the knowledge of good and evil, is to sit at Lucifer's table; to partake of his evil works, or to do his bidding at the expense of obedience to our God - The God of Abraham, the God of Isaac and the God of Jacob. It is important to note that humanity has the freedom to choose, and the penalty for disobedience is clearly given - death.

Genesis 3:1-7 indicates how Lucifer, playing on the emotions of humanity and openly lying in order to be effective in his deception, is able to present death, the same penalty for disobedience to God, as a very attractive option for humanity. The sad fact is that 9.5 out of 10 times Lucifer is successful at his craft. This is why the Israelite scripture states that the serpent was more subtle than any beast of the field which God had made. He was able to convince the woman (Eve) by telling her, **"Ye shall not surely die; for God doth know that in the day ye eat thereof, then your eyes shall be opened, and ye shall be as gods, knowing good and evil."**

Today the role of this woman is played by the men of Freemasonry, Christianity and Khazarism or Judaism. Most of these men foolishly entertain female demons and other earth-bound spirits and thus help to create an environment for homosexuality. During the masonic initiation, the candidate is blindfolded and led by a blue rope tied around his neck. The blindfold is called a "hoodwink" and the rope a "cabletow". Just consider the implications of these symbolic acts.

The disciples of the serpent who were secretly initiated into the rites of the serpent seemed to benefit most physically.

They, like the Pharaoh, the Priesthood and the elite controlled the levels of power in the ancient world, profiting immensely at the expense of others. To be initiated into the rites of the serpent is to make a covenant with Lucifer; to worship in his synagogue and rebel against God. Such people find the fruit of the tree of good and evil to be desirable and most pleasant to eat. They also claim to be like gods, to be illuminated by possessing secret and forbidden knowledge. Such people secretly wear the apron of shame and damnation with great pride and pomp, unlike Adam and Eve, who wore it as a symbol of their disgrace, disobedience and damnation. Wearing the apron is the trademark of masonry. It is considered to be their symbol of innocence. Yet all these heathens are prisoners of their own philosophy, being deceived by their own master, as that old serpent weaves his seductive magic, casting spells of blindness over his unsuspecting victims, who continue to lust after his fruit.

This man, this tree, this serpent, this chief spirit of evil, is extremely good at what he does, possessing tremendous spiritual power. He should never be underestimated, because to do such would be to blindly fall prey to his craftiness. This same serpent, who inspired the woman to disobey the law or command of the God of the Israelites, and subsequently to coerce her husband also into disobedience, this same serpent was openly worshipped by the ancient Egyptians and Babylonians.

WHOREMONGERS

Let us investigate some of the basic characteristics of the Great Whore in order to be better prepared to defend ourselves against her seduction. First of all, the fabric of the Great Whore is so intriguingly woven, that it is extremely difficult to determine the specific boundaries of the three Orders of Khazarism, Freemasonry and Christianity. Therefore, to address one is to address all; e.g. Mr. Adam Weishaupt, the founder of the masonic Order of the Illuminati, was a Khazarian Christian priest; and Mr. Karl Marx, the spokesman for whoredom, was Khazarian raised as a Christian. The one characteristic that always remain constant, however, is that these disciples of the Great Whore are all Gentile heathens, regardless of what they may want to call themselves. As may be seen from the fruits of their labour, the ways of the Gentile should be resisted. In addition, it is quite evident that the deceptive philosophy of Khazarism, or Yiddishism, or Judaism as it is commonly called, is at the forefront of the culture of the Great Whore.

The other two philosophies of Freemasonry and Christianity are merely instruments or vehicles which are manipulated by the Gentile Khazars. Khazarism itself is a very complex Order, consisting of Judaism, Bolshevism, Marxism, Communism and Socialism. All these "isms" have a secret side that is only visible with a good understanding of Khazarism. Since Mr. Karl Marx typifies the nature of Khazarism in socialism, and we shall examine the hidden side of its many characters.

The popular Karl Heinrich Marx was a Gentile Khazarian born in Trier, Rhineland, Germany in 1818 and whose real name was Kissel Mordekay. Isn't this typical of the Khazars to call themselves by another name in order to hide their true identity? Mr. Marx was a freeloader, relying on his rich friend Mr. Engels to support him for almost the entire duration of his adult life, rather than work for an honest living. Isn't this just a little strange for a man who claimed to be the champion of the oppressed and down trodden worker? What does he know about work? Today we have the Khazarian impostor freeloading by riding on the coat-tails of the Israelites. As a so-called anti-capitalist, Marx's livelihood, by way of Engels, was derived mainly from the blood, sweat and tears of children, who slaved in a cotton mill of Lancashire, England, owned by Engels father. In addition, Marx the "anti-capitalist", traded profitably on the London Stock Exchange. Is this the same man who claimed to be the champion of the working class against the "exploiting capitalist"? We have all seen the Khazarian logo with one paw on the globe, yet they insist on swinging the "incest" pot at the altar. Don't they know that whoremongers and dogs are excluded from the city of God? Finally, Marx showed vicious contempt for his own family when he allowed two of his six children to die of starvation. This he did either because he refused to work to support his family, being a freeloader, or no one would hire him. Either way he hated work, yet wanted to live like the bourgeois, which he pretended to reject in public. This evil attitude drove two of his other children to commit suicide. How wretched! How wicked ! How Khazarian!

It is an historical fact that Freemasonry as practised today, i.e. speculative masonry with all its symbolism and deception, was founded on the principles of Khazarism. It was the elite of the Gentile Khazar, who dominated the banking industry of the western Gentiles while preaching socialism, communism and Judaism, that orchestrated the Protestant Christians in 1717 to re-organize Freemasonry. This re-structuring, complete with a new code of conduct, cleverly gave the Khazars the upper hand since they had already designed the coat-of-arms for Freemasonry and later the official masonic seal used on the diplomas of each degree. This Gentile Khazarian has stolen from the Israelites of Iberia (Spain/Portugal), also called the Moors or black Jews, corrupting their teachings after the Israelites were expelled to the Western Sudan (West Africa) in the late 15th century. Thus the Israelite doctrine became perverted in the hands of the Khazars and evolved into what is now called Judaism and Kabbalah, or simply Khazarism. It was on this deceptive philosophy of Khazarism that the rituals of Freemasonry, or Liberalism were founded. Liberalism is the definition of the "New Christianity"; also known as "Liberation Theology" in its mild state and "New Age" in the extreme. It is interesting to note that the official publication of the Supreme Council (33rd degree) of Freemasonry is also called "New Age". The goal of the Liberals, however, was to create a Godless society, where Lucifer would have free reign. The fact that the Khazars spitefully call themselves "Jews" also helped their alliance with Christianity and the evil plot to have Gentiles dominate Israelite culture, by falsely claiming ownership of the Bible so that God would appear white. Do not be fooled by their public display of antagonism, it is just an act for the television cameras; but observe their deeds instead. Where there is no camera, the play is on emotion. The trick is to talk about lots of love, but no truth.

THE ADULTERY OF THE CHILDREN OF SLAVERY

The brunt of the repression of the Great Whore has been borne by God's elect - the Children of Slavery. Yet these same Children of Slavery who call themselves Muslims are just as ridiculous as those who call themselves Christians. I was shocked to hear a so-called black nationalist Islamic leader, expressed on a popular television talk show, how he entertained Khazarians (he called them Jews) at his palatial home. This is the same man, who every chance he gets, tries to put down these same people. I found it very strange indeed, until I discovered in my research that every Shriner must kneel before the Koran and take his oath in the name of Allah, acknowledging that pagan Mohammedan god as his god. This helped to explain the dress of the Shriner, with his fez and sword; but more importantly, the Shriners are only selected from the 32nd Degree Masons - the very cream of the top of Freemasonry. Furthermore, everybody knows that a shrine is a tomb and a place where the dead is worshipped, just like the pyramids and the so-called Christian church. However, whether this same Muslim leader is a Shriner or a Mason is not clear, but the fact is that there is a very strong link between Islam, Freemasonry, Christianity and Khazarism. When the Gentile enslaves us on his own, it may be excused since that is his role; but when a child of slavery joins with the Gentile to help enslave another child of slavery, that is treachery, and such a traitor is inexcusable.

Then there is the other so-called black nationalist Christian, who in his last election campaign, insulted the same Khazarians. Obviously he lost his bid for election, thanks mainly to the efforts of the Khazarian Mayor of New York City at that time. This same man was practically wedded to the aforementioned Islamic leader, refusing to separate himself despite pressure to do so. Today one cannot help but notice his jowl (the area from the cheek to the throat). Usually pigs have a jowl, as do politicians. Could he too be drinking from the same trough as the Khazarians, at the expense of his own people?

This accusation has been made by those in a position to know; but it is much more important to recognize the depth and power of the Great Whore. Even black nationalism or Pan-Africanism may just be a front for the manifestation of the Great Whore. Pan-Africanism was founded on the foundation of socialism which in turn is based on paganism.

It is extremely important to understand that "Pan-Africanism" is not African or black nationalism. First of all, **every nation must demonstrate a sense of spiritual unity**; this is the foundation of all nationalities, whether understood or not. Such a foundation is lacking among Africans, the Children of Slavery or black people generally. Thus all those shouting "Pan-Africanism" continue to be the laughing stock of the world. How can anybody take them seriously? They are all drunk with the wine of the Great Whore - the wine of damnation. Pan-Africanism is a poor attempt by black people, who lack understanding, to imitate the culture or philosophy of the white Gentile pagan.

This philosophy, just like Pan-Americanism, has its roots in Pan-Germanism or German Imperialism, as seen by Freemasonry since the days of the Order of the Illuminati. Karl Marx was just a tool for Khazarism, as the mouth-piece for its platform of socialism or Bolshevism. Expressed another way, this socialist idea was just another attempt of subversive activity by an elite few, in order to achieve world domination. Where do you think Hitler got his ideas from? Again we have come full circle, in order to show how the Great Whore has deceptively dominated our philosophical thinking through the idea of Pan-Africanism. This is called mental slavery and is more effective than yokes or guns, since the victims of this deception represent the brilliant minds of the upper class among the Children of Slavery. They in turn influence the masses and the disciples of Lucifer knock glasses of Cognac for a job well done.

THE GENTILE ORIGINS OF WHOREDOM

The pagan origins of Christianity may be proven historically. Even in the Holy Bible, the sacred book of the Israelites, the fact that there is no reference to Christianity clearly indicates that this Gentile philosophy is not of the God of Truth. Moreover, just observe the practises of a Christian and then try to find the precedence in the holy scriptures; it will never be found. In fact, the two doctrines contradict each other, yet the Christians read from the Israelite holy scriptures. How is this possible? Has it ever occurred to you that Christianity has a secret or hidden meaning behind the words that are read from the Israelite New Testament? Why would anyone with the slightest degree of common sense believe in the pagan doctrine of Christianity? Did the people with whom our God made the first covenant change from those with whom He made the new one? NO! Read Heb. 8:1-13. Did the scriptures ever say that salvation would cease from among the Jews [Israelites] and be given to the Christians? NO! Did Jesus the Christ ever say that his followers would be called "Christians". NO! This statement was made by man, and a pagan man at that. So where or what is the problem? Let us examine the hidden mysteries of Christianity and expose this side of the Great Whore for the lie that it is.

During the time of Paul, that famous Israelite who is practically worshipped by Christians today, Israelites then were rudely called "Christians" by the Gentile Romans, as a very derogatory nickname. The situation was not unlike today where the descendants of the same Israelites are called "nigger" or "Negro", by the descendants of the same Gentile pagans. Thus, in keeping with the sequence of events, the pagan Gentiles will one day soon be calling themselves "niggers" or "Negroes" and surrounding the name with a new philosophy. However, by the year 312 A.D., among the Gentile Romans, idolatry was no longer considered to be paganism, since it was called by its new name "Christianity", thanks to Constantine; but by then most Israelites had fled to Western Sudan (West Africa) to avoid Roman persecution. It was simply a case of "if you can't beat them, join them", because despite the Roman persecutions, the Gentile followers of the Israelites refused to surrender their faith. This deceptive act by the pagan Constantine allowed the practise of paganism to continue under a new name and marked a new era in the behaviour of the Great Whore.

These "new" pagan rites under the name of Christianity were known as "arcani disciplina", or secret discipline and excluded the uninitiated. Now how were the initiated recognized from the other Christians? Simply by making the sign of the cross on the chest, that was the secret signal. Obviously the followers of the Israelites would not have known anything about the cross as a secret symbol. Only those who knew of the secret signal would gain access to the temple. We must understand that the cross was not openly displayed as it is today until about 692. Within the temples, the initiate had to be baptised in water, (backward of course) and would be marked with the secret sign of the cross on his forehead, just as babies are done today in Christianity. How sinful! This practise of initiation is purely Babylonian, while the wearing of the cross in the form of an earring or suspended from a necklace is uniquely Egyptian. Purification consisted of sprinkling with pig's blood, which was also used to invoke familiar evil spirits.

In another ritual, the death of the sun-god was depicted in the slaying of a male child, which was said to represent Jesus. The blood of the dead child was drunk and his body eaten. Today the Christian priest uses wine [blood] and a round wafer [sun], while talking about the last supper of Jesus the Christ. How clever! In Babylonia, where this pagan ritual originated, it was performed in worship of their god Baal. Thus the priest was called "Khana-Baal" or "Cahna-Baal", meaning the priest of Baal; hence the word "cannibal". **Now we know that a true cannibal is a pagan Christian Gentile priest who performs their**

ritual of communion. This ritual may be compared with the initiation of the 33rd degree mason at the Temple of the Supreme Council of the Thirty-Third and Last Degree of the Ancient and Accepted Scottish Rite, in Washington, D.C. This temple may be aptly called the Temple of the Serpent, not because there is a large cobra wrapped around the neck of one of the two sphinxes at the entrance; nor the six large snakes in the stone work high over the entrance; nor because the inner walls are decorated with serpents of various kinds; but simply the fact that wine is drunk from a human skull at their altar, to seal the oath of the Sovereign Grand Inspector General.

The spirit of the Great Whore is so complex that it would take a life time to illustrate and even then, with the numerous secret Orders within secret Orders, it is impossible for any investigative researcher, inside or outside, to fully determine its identity. What matters most, however, is that we become aware and not be fooled. The entire world is presently awaiting the re-birth of the Nation of the Lost Tribes of House of Israel and the return of their Messiah. The fact that everyone is waiting on the resurrection of the Children of Slavery is clear evidence of the identity of God's elect. There is no other gate through which salvation may be achieved. Yet the entire world is also awaiting the incarnation of the spirit of the infamous Anti-Christ, who would appear as an Israelite born among us but not of us but is placed there to deceive. **I John 2:18-19** "...They went out from us, but they were not of us; for if they had been of us, they would no doubt have continued with us: but they went out, that they might be made manifest that they were not all of us." He too has his elect, the deceivers of this world. We have seen how efficient and effective they can be, from the days of ancient Egypt until now. The Christian teachers who speak evil on new age, freemasonry, KKK, and others are very ignorant or otherwise looking for a fast buck. They are pigs fighting against pigs in the same mud under the same banner of Christianity. The children of slavery, within the bowels of Christianity, will eventually produce the Anti-Christ, while the philosophy itself will be representative of the Great Whore. Be ye not deceived!

THE OBELISK

From the beginning of time, man had always associated the standing stone with the act of worship. The power and majesty of the natural mountains of stone has always fascinated the ancient mind, especially the ability to withstand the onslaught of the elements and time, and the capacity to belch fire and molten rock. Thus, it was no coincidence that the ancient man also associated the spirits or gods with the standing stone. Indeed, our Father, the God of the Israelites, is often referred to in the Israelite scriptures as "The Rock". Of course, where else would our brother Moses seek water [Num. 20:7-11], but from The Rock?

Who else can create water from nothing? We can say then that a stone is not a stone, neither are all rocks equal. It is simply a matter of who you call upon; or more importantly who instructs you concerning the rock or stone. Furthermore, neither Moses nor our forefathers worshipped the standing stone; yet they all used the stones to build altars in order to worship our God. It is this mystery of bowing down before the standing stone(s) that we shall explore.

Among the ancient Egyptians, it was widely believed that the gods or spirits dwelt within the standing stone. As a result, certain stones which happened to be present when an important event occurred, were deemed sacred and were reverenced because they were considered to have favourable influences. This in turn led to stone-worship, since the magical or spiritual powers generated from bowing down before a standing stone became too seductive to resist. Soon sacrifices and gifts were offered, along with prayers and praises. Needless to say, these actions attracted even more familiar and evil spirits to the stone, However, since the standing stone became so valuable to the ancient Egyptian, it was necessary to devote much care and attention to it. Where this stone was not readily available, quarries were started and it was hewed from its natural environment and transported to a location of special prominence. There it was used to entertain the spirits, who were then worshipped. It was from these specially hewed and decorated stones that the Obelisk originated. At this point it will be necessary to contrast the instructions given by the God of the Israelites regarding the Israelite altar of stone. Ex. 20:24-25 specifically states that no hewed stones were to be used to build that altar, since the altar would be considered polluted if so built. From whom then did the Egyptians get their instructions?

Let us consider for a moment the classic case of that Egyptian pagan sect, the Mohammedans, who continue even to this very day to bow down in worship, before a black stone of the Kaaba in Mecca. Every year millions of Mohammedans insist on making the pilgrimage to Mecca, trampling one another to death, like cattle on a stampede, just to worship a piece of stone that somebody said fell from heaven. Yet the Mohammedans were not the first to worship a black stone because the Zoroastrians did the same. Is it possible then that all these sincere people simply lack the spirit of understanding?

The fact that the black stone fell from heaven should indicate that there was something wrong with it, even though it may possess certain extraordinary qualities. Anyone with the spirit of understanding would have known that a certain "stone" was casted out from heaven a long time ago. That same stone used to be associated with the Great and Almighty Rock, but became tarnished and was thrown down to the earth. Today this is the stone that is worshipped throughout the entire world, whether in the form of a black stone, an obelisk, a cross, or a pyramid, it remains a source of power and knowledge for this evil and perverted world. Even the pagan Gentile Christians had their own black stone, over which their priests engaged in homosexual rituals, as part of their acts of worship, skillfully timing their orgasms to coincide with the ringing of the bells of their Gothic cathedral while worshipping their god, then called Elegabalus, which was another name for the sun god in Antioch. How disgusting! How evil!

Also in ancient Egypt, it was the custom to ensure that after the death of an important member of the community, spiritual ties with that individual should continue, so that others may benefit from his wisdom or benevolence. Thus a funerary monument or stone was established to commemorate the deceased and also to be used for the invocation of the spirit of that individual. Herein lies the origin of the popular tombstone and the evil practise of ancestral worship or voodoo. This is precisely the reason why the Gentile pagans, especially the Christians, built their places of worship in the cemetery so that they may worship the dead comfortably. In fact, some of the V.I.P.'s of Christianity were buried under the floor of their place of worship, mainly under the altar, for a greater spiritual impact. Where this was not possible, the building itself was erected on a grave site.

In this we know that the "Jesus" of Christianity is not the same as Jesus the Christ of the Israelites, because in Matt. 22:29-32, Jesus the Christ, stated that as touching the resurrection of the dead, they are in error, not knowing the scriptures, nor the power of God, Furthermore, he stated that God, The God of Abraham, The God of Isaac and The God of Jacob, is not the God of the dead, but of the living; also see Mark 12: 24-27 and Luke 20:34-38.

The funerary stone evolved into the Ben stone, which was a short standing stone with a thick base and the top tapered into a point. The Egyptians believed that the spirit of the sun resided in the Ben stone and became visible in the form of a bird called the Benu; hence the name of the stone. This bird was considered to be the spirit of their god Ra and also of Osiris. The Gentile Greeks identified the Benu with the Phoenix and their American descendants with the eagle. Eventually the shaft of the Ben or Sun stone was lengthened to form what the Egyptians called "Tekhen" or "Tekhenu"; the same is called the Obelisk today. It was erected in pairs, in honour of the sun-god Ra or Amon-Ra, in order to obtain from him the gift of eternal life. These sun-stones were erected at the entrance of temples and shrines, with their tapered top, or pyramidion, shaped to represent the rays of the sun, spreading wider as they reach the earth.

Along with the worshipping of the dead and the sun was the worshipping of the phallus or penis. Just as the rays of the masculine sun penetrated the womb (soil) of mother earth, causing the seed to be fertilized and giving life to plants, the erect phallus of a man (obelisk) was also capable of giving life after sexual union with a woman. In other words, the male reproductive organ was worshipped as the creator of life. Needless to say, the shape of the obelisk is in the shape of an erect penis. In Christianity the same phallus is called a spire or steeple; in the Oriental culture it is called a pagoda and among the Mohammedans it is called a minaret. Many Christians may be shocked to learn of these facts and may want to close their ears to the truth. The choice is theirs to make; but the British Government has documented proof that sexual images were found under the altars of about 90% of all the so-called Christian churches throughout England. This they found when they undertook to inspect buildings damaged by air raids after the second Gentile war, otherwise known as W.W. II. Yet there is more! Have you ever seen the picture of the "Hagia Sophia"? This deception of the Christian goddess of wisdom is in the subliminal image of the female reproductive organ. I just could not believe my eyes when I saw such explicit details so skillfully designed. But then Christianity is the root of deception. So what else is new? Look at the way they took over the Bible, allowing people to believe that it is a Christian book.

When I received a copy of a Christian magazine, depicting their "Lady of Guadalupe" on the cover there it was again, the same image of the female reproductive organ. Could all this emphasis on perverted sexuality be real, or am I just imagining things? Before you answer, remember that the hidden doctrine of Christianity is found among the Freemasons, and guess who built the Gothic cathedrals throughout Europe, the same ones with the sexual images under the altars. Therefore, let us look at their symbol of identity and the manner in which it is portrayed.

The compass (male) is alway shown straddling the square (female) and right in the centre of these two instruments is the big "G". These items are said to be the tools of the "Grand Architect of the Universe", whom most people would assume is God, but this is not the case. The "G" is symbolic of the generative principle, which is the same as the phallus or male organ of procreation. Now just think of what occurred in the Garden of Eden between Lucifer and Eve and the consequences thereof, then put it all together for yourself.

A NATION IN TURMOIL

How is it that a people who were once so mighty could have fallen so low? How could a nation of Princes and Princesses be transformed into gangs of slaves? They conquered Egypt and ruled her from Avaris in the delta of Goshen for over 200 years, forming the XVth and XVIth Dynasties. They defeated Thutmose III, one of ancient Egypt's most powerful kings, during their glorious exodus from that country. **They established the ancient kingdom of Israel** holding the balance of power between Egypt and Babylonia. **They wrote the book on morality and ethics; the book which has become the standard of truth; the book which today is known as the Holy Bible.** Even in their state of disarray, they were still able to bring civilization to Western Europe, using their superior biblical philosophy, and also built the splendid West African Empires of Ghana, Mali and Songhai. So where did we go wrong? Just look at our deplorable state today. How do we rebuild this powerful, black nation?

Today we are a lost nation living in the lands of our captivity, in a state of mental slavery, without the knowledge of our true identity. How did we manage to lose our superior Israelite identity? How do we explain this present state of mental slavery? Many of us would want to deny that we wear the shackles of mental slavery. But such a denial is a clear sign of slavery itself; nothing but complacency, a broken or suppressed spirit, a willingness to be satisfied with the crumbs from the master's table. We have become like a drunk man, who argues against his drunkenness, because he has lost that mental ability to discern his natural state of perfect balance. Yet he continues to slur in his speech and trips over his shadow. We should not fool ourselves, regardless of how loud we shout our Afrocentric ideology, our mentality

remains Eurocentric. Whose philosophy are we applying?
What cultural values do we express? What ever happened to our original Israelite philosophy and culture?
Before we can begin the healing process, we must first rid our mind of the excess baggage. We might as well forget about ancient Egypt because the white man was first in line for her spoils, and **when we understand that Ancient Egypt was and still is our biggest enemy, we should not care to be re-acquainted.**

  The white man has stolen the spirit of Ancient Egypt and makes good use of it today to suppress us. He took the obelisk, the pyramid, the eye of Horus and their queen of heaven - Isis. All these have now become the very foundation of his culture - his "religion", philosophy, politics, economics, etc. But this should not come as any surprise, since our Prophets of old taught that this would actually happen. We did not listen then and we still refuse to listen today. Woe unto us! There is only one way to obtain the power of the ancient Egyptians and that power would not work for us like it would for the white man anyway. We would have to be initiated in the Greater Mysteries of Osiris and the Lesser Mysteries of Isis. But who would be our Hierophant? Do we really think that the white man would share the "sacred word" with us? **Remember, we defeated Egypt before, at the height of her power, with the Greatest General of all time and Moses as His Lieutenant, and we must do it again.**

Contrary to popular opinion, there is only one truth, even though that same truth may be manifested in various ways. Thus the truth and the lie are opposite forces with separate and different identities, because to deceive is to lie. Now then, which side are we on and how do we know? This is extremely important because in order to rebuild our nation, we must all walk the same spiritual path. The next step should be to sever all spiritual ties with the philosophy of the New Egypt. This may not be easy since it means discarding a philosophy and cultural values which are the very essence of our existence, that have become ingrained within our minds during the last 375 years.

Let us now research the book of our forefathers in order to understand this mess in which we now find ourselves. **Genesis 15:13 explains that we would be strangers in a land that is not ours and we shall serve a nation which would afflict us for 400 years.** The slave trade to this New Egypt started around 1619, which means the period of slavery will soon end, but only for those who are prepared to end it. Just to set the record straight, 430 years were spent by us in the old Egypt [Exodus 12:40]. **Deut. 28:32 states, "Thy sons and thy daughters shall be given unto another people, and thine eyes shall look, and fail with longing for them all the day long, and there shall be no might in thine hands."** Later we shall see how the black Muslims sold us into slavery to the white Christians. **Deut. 28:36 reads, "The Lord shall bring thee, and thy king which thou shalt set over thee, unto a nation which neither thou nor thy fathers have known; and there shalt thou SERVE OTHER GODS, wood and stone."** Well there can be no denying that we are here and are serving other gods; yet some of us still have those regal characteristics.

Deut. 28:48 says, "Therefore shalt thou serve thine enemies which the Lord shall send against thee, in hunger, and in thirst, and in nakedness, and in want of all things: and he shall put a YOKE OF IRON UPON

THY NECK, until he has destroyed thee." Go to your local library and see who wore the yoke of iron around their necks. Now remember this verse next Sunday as you attend the Christian church service, only substitute "mind" for "neck". Finally, for the die-hard there is **Deut. 28:68, "And the Lord shall bring thee INTO EGYPT AGAIN WITH SHIPS,...and THERE YE SHALL BE SOLD UNTO YOUR ENEMIES FOR BONDMEN AND BONDWOMEN..."**

Note this will be our second trip into Egypt and this time by ship, obviously with the yoke around our necks. Remember, we used to walk to and from Egypt in the past, so is this a symbolic Egypt? Well partly so! But consider the following facts:

1) At "St. Peter's" Basilica in Rome, standing 83 feet tall, is the Vatican obelisk re-erected by Pope Sixtus V in 1586 in order to **exalt the mysteries of the Christian philosophy.** Above the pyramidion on the top of the obelisk is the emblem of the Christian sun-god and above that the symbol of death - the dreaded cross. These two Christian mystery symbols were added in Rome. This obelisk was brought from Heliopolis [the sun city] in EGYPT around 39 A.D. by Emperor Gaius or Caligula.

2) At the Piazza of "St. John" Lateran in Rome is a 105 feet obelisk taken from the temple of Amon-Ra at Karnak, EGYPT. It was commissioned by Thothmes [Thutmose] III and raised by his grandson Thutmose IV [1425-1417 B.C.]. It was Constantine who first decided to transfer it to New Rome or Constantinople in 330 A.D., but died before he could complete the task. His successor, Constantius brought the obelisk to Rome in 357. It was re-erected in 1588 and dedicated to the "Invincible Cross" by Pope Sixtus V.

3) At the Place de la Concorde in Paris, France stands a 75 foot obelisk from the temple at Luxor, EGYPT. It was one of two erected by Rameses II around 1285 B.C. In 1830, as the French Minister of Public Works, Louis Thiers approved the transfer from Luxor. In 1836 when it was erected in Paris, Mr. Thiers was the Prime Minister and in 1871 he became the first President of France. Coincidence?

4) On the banks of the River Thames in London, England is an obelisk from the temple of Harakhthes at Heliopolis, EGYPT. It used to be one of two erected by Thutmose III and was first moved to Alexandria by Augustus Caesar around 13 B.C. It was re-erected in 1878 at its present site and stands 68.5 feet tall.

5) In New York's Central Park, across from the Metropolitan Museum is the other obelisk, which was previously erected by Thutmose III at Heliopolis, EGYPT. It was also first moved by Augustus Caesar and finally arrived in New York in 1880.

We are all familiar with the Washington Monument and other obelisks, of which there are many. But the key to this whole mystery is understanding the purpose for having these monoliths. Briefly **they were used by the Ancient Egyptians to worship the sun-god Amon-Ra or Ra/Re and to entertain the spirits of the deceased, which they called gods** - ["Ra" is the Hebrew word for evil]. In the Egyptian Mystery System, every Pharaoh was considered to be the son of the sun-god Re/Ra, so **they erected the obelisk in honour of the sun-god in order to obtain its favour of POWER and eternal life.** When the obelisk was transferred to another country that was initiated into the Egyptian Mysteries, and all

Western nations have, the spirits of Egyptian gods simply moved with it, since the initiated had to worship these gods. What was one of the first things Alexander did when the Greeks arrived in Egypt? He headed straight for the Grand Lodge of Luxor to obtain the knowledge of the Egyptian Mysteries. Then he set himself up as a god. In the case of the Romans, after learning the Mysteries, they realized that they could have the POWER of Egypt without the headaches of colonization. The process was called Christianity and was based on the Egyptian system. All they had to do was to capture the tools of the trade and the POWER would be a their disposal. Does it really work? Just look around today and see who is wielding the POWER, then observe their customs.

But what does all this have to do with us? Well go back to Deut. 28:68 again, now pause and think. Does it all come together now? **The same spirit of oppression used in Ancient Egypt by the Pharaohs, is being used today by the Christians who bought us from the black Muslims, to keep us enslaved.** Remember the words of Pope Sixtus V, who spoke very clearly in 1586 as he dedicated the Vatican obelisk to the exaltation of the mysteries of Christianity; and he was the king of all Christianity. Sixtus V re-erected five obelisks, more than any other Roman Christian, so he must have known something. Notice also that the obelisk is usually situated close to the major seat of POWER, e.g. the Washington Monument being across the street from the White House.

They may also be cleverly woven into the design of the building housing POWER, e.g. the Parliament Buildings of Canada and England. Many Christian church buildings are similarly designed and miniature ones are also found in cemeteries of old Christian church buildings. Now it becomes quite clear that there is no difference between "church and state". The Christian Mysteries is just an extension of a bigger Mystery System, which all leads back to Egypt, which in turn leads back to Babylonia. But how do we know that this system is wrong for us?

First of all, it does not, and will not, work for us as Israelites. Why? Simply because it is structured against us - our culture, philosophy and religion. All others may benefit, but not us. Sure there is Michael Jackson and Bill Cosby, but who else! How many thousands do they employ? Secondly, to understand better we have to examine the word "Obelisk". Many West Indians will recognize the first syllable "obe" or "ob" from the word "obeah". "Ob" or "Oub" is also the name of the Egyptian serpent-god and serpent-worship, fire-worship and sun-worship are synonymous.

[To gain a better understanding of this matter, read THE WORD, THE ISRAELITES AND THE DAMNED, edited by Shadrock.] The second syllable is "belisk" which relates to a fire-breathing reptile. In the book of Isaiah (30:6) it is referred to as "the beast of the south" [Egypt] and also the "fiery flying serpent". Today we have "basilisk", or "basilica", meaning the house of the serpent - [consider the Basilica of the Vatican]. Therefore, today's "obeah-man" is not an old, big foot black man living in poverty, but rather an intelligent white Gentile male, dressed in an expensive suit or long, black robe with a big cross, and living like a king. **Now we should go to the book written by our forefathers to see who this fire-breathing reptile really is. Revelation chapter 12 identifies the reptile as Lucifer or Satan, the god of death and enemy of our God. Chapter 17 describes the wife of Lucifer (Christianity) - the Great Whore, together they are called "The Beast", which drinks the blood of Israelites.** This is why the present Mystery System of Christianity and Islam is great for our enemies, but deadly for us as Israelites.

Now that there is a better understanding of the system, let us review the historical process in order to see how we lost our culture and our superior philosophy. Between 622 and 708 the Muslim philosophy and culture known as Islam, which originated in Egypt with the Ishmaelites, swept Northern Africa. Our ancestors who resided chiefly at Cyrenaica, Mauritania and Numidia, after their dispersal from Ancient Israel, were decimated. Many fled across the Sahara to West Africa to avoid the violence of these Muslims and Arabs. It is quite clear from this historical fact that Islam is not our original culture or philosophy. **In fact, the Muslims like the ancient Egyptians, are our enemies, since Ishmael, the father of the Muslims, was the son of an Egyptian woman; married an Egyptian and grew up in Egyptian culture.** They have displaced us, those whom they did not murder they enslaved and therefore aided in our being a lost nation without knowledge of self. But this was only the beginning, later they would strike again with the same deadly consequences.

In 1478 the Christian infidels of Spain, led by King Ferdinand and Queen Isabella, established the Spanish Inquisition. This secret, evil institution was the first stage of persecution designed by the Christians to force the expulsion of our ancestors from Spain. Many of our ancestors were murdered or tortured, while others had their properties confiscated. On March 31, 1492 Ferdinand and Isabella finally issued a decree expelling all our ancestors from Spain. The majority found temporary refuge in Portugal, where they joined others already there, while others fled to Northern Africa. **The predominant Muslim community of North Africa rejected our ancestors causing many to**

perish. Meanwhile, the Christians of Portugal were engaging in their own persecutions similar to the Spanish. In 1484, King Joao II, started to forcibly convert our ancestors to Christianity. Those who refused were shipped to St. Thomas or San Thome, just off the coast of West Africa. Finally, in 1496, King Manoel issued a decree expelling all our ancestors from Portugal. Again many would find a sanctuary among their brethren of Western Africa.

It should be quite obvious by now who our real enemies are - "Christianity and Islam", one white and the other black. Those of us who continue to look strictly at the colour issue may want to take a second look. We are observing a systematic destruction of our cultural heritage, which in time has made us forget who we really are and what our responsibility is supposed to be. Every time one of our ancestors was killed or displaced we lost that knowledge of self. Such heart wrenching and traumatic experiences are enough to cause us to forget our very names, and we did. **We referred to our selves as Blacks, Afro-this and African-that, Negro, etc., anything but Israelites. But such was the plan of Lucifer from the beginning - read Psalm 83 in our history book.** However, we were made stronger than other nations [Gen. 25:23] and it would take much more than murder and displacement to bring us down, so we started to build again.

As early as 790 the wealth and splendour of the Empire of Ghana was common knowledge world wide. Its education system was second only to that of Egypt, and the main centre at Timbuctu predated those of Europe by about one thousand years.
By this time forty-four Israelite kings had reigned in Ghana. But in 1076 along came those nasty Muslims again. This time the infidels known as the ALMORAVIDS raped and

plundered Ghana at will. They insisted on the conversion to their cult and since they controlled the external trade routes, the elite of Ghana found it expedient to fall in line. From that time onwards Western Africa was never the same. The infusion of the alien Muslim culture and philosophy disrupted the normal peaceful way of life which our ancestors led previously. Ghana gave way to Mali, which in turn was replaced by Songhai. Finally, along came the Muslims again in 1591 and effectively put an end to the Empire of Songhai and the prosperity of Western Africa. This weakening of our forefathers by the Muslims paved the way for our eventual mass enslavement.

Due to information received from Muslim traders, the Christians of Portugal learnt of **"the People of the Book", or as the Muslims called them "Yehudi", meaning "Jew or Israelite"**, who were living in great numbers to the south of the Sahara; a race cursed of God and predestined as slaves. On this valuable tip and armed with the blessings of their Pope, the deadly cross and the sword, the pagan Christians with the gleam of greed in their eyes sailed for the shores of Western Africa. By 1500 the Muslims were firmly in control of Western Africa and these black vultures had started the odious act of rounding up our ancestors like cattle and selling them as slaves to the white Christians. **But we should not be alarmed, because in the book of our forefathers it says in Genesis 39:1. "And Joseph was brought down to Egypt; and Potiphar, an officer of Pharaoh, captain of the guard, an Egyptian, bought him of the hands of the Ishmaelites, which had brought him down thither."** Thus the spirit of our forefathers will remain restless and angry, as long as we continue to embrace the pagan philosophies and cultures of their enemies, through the adoption of Christianity and Islam. Even after we arrived in the lands of our present captivity, the spirit of our forefathers tried to inform us through songs of our true identity and our original philosophy and culture. **Remember the old "Negro Spirituals!"** This majestic musical experience is yet unsurpassed or unequalled. It is very interesting to listen to the words of these songs of the slaves. There was nothing sung about the Nile, Sphinx, Pyramids, Mecca, Sahara, Niger or Congo. Yet all these were well known, especially the West African locations. Neither did the slaves sing about "Ramadan", "Good Friday", "Easter", or even "Christmas". **Instead the slaves sang about Moses, Pharaoh's drowning in the Red Sea; Joshua's tumbling of the walls of Jericho; the Hebrew Children and their old time religion, Jacob's ladder; Ezekiel's vision of the wheel [cherubim]; Daniel's vision of the stone made without hands; Nebuchadnezzar and the hand writing on the wall; the Promised Land; the River Jordan; the Sabbaths and Zion.**

Do not forget that these same slaves were being taught every Sunday by the white Christian master from the New Testament. Yet practically all their songs were of the Old Testament. The white Christian slave master did not and still does not understand the bible. If he did he would have followed the instructions therein. By now it should be crystal clear that the majestic musical experience was **the oppressed spirit of THE NATION OF THE LOST TRIBES OF THE HOUSE OF ISRAEL crying out to his God, THE GOD OF ABRAHAM, THE GOD OF ISAAC AND THE GOD OF JACOB, for mercy and salvation.**

CURSE OF SLAVERY

The institution of serfdom has been around almost as long as humanity. When ever there was war the captives were usually subject to serfdom of one sort or another. Throughout ancient Africa serfs generally form an integral part of the society, the lowest level. One may become a serf in order to pay off debts, or by contractual arrangement.

The serf or servant may be considered a part of his master's family and sometimes even marry his master's daughter or inherit some of his wealth. However, it would be in Europe, amongst the Slavic lands, that we must start the story of "slavery". Between the 8th and 11th centuries, during the growth and expansion of Islam, the Slavic tribes of Central and Eastern Europe accounted for the vast majority of the slaves throughout the world. The slaves or Slavs formed an important component of the Islamic commercial system, although they were mainly used as artisans, domestics and soldiers. Despite all this, none of the horrors of the last or most recent slave system were ever experienced. This system of slavery was unique in three major ways.

It was the first time that an entire nation was enslaved - all Israelites. It was the first time that the transportation of the captives was done exclusively by ships [Deut. 28:68]; and thirdly, the entire experience, horror and all, was foretold and recorded, by the Prophets of the captives, some three thousand years earlier [Gen. 15:13-14; Deut. 28]. Let us then reference the ancient record of our Israelite forefathers in order to understand this curse of slavery, in which most of us still find ourselves.
First of all we should ask, Why slavery? In order to answer this question, we must have some knowledge of self; but even if we

do not have access to that knowledge, we must see slavery as a curse, as opposed to a blessing. So what is a curse? A curse is a spiritual invocation in order to cause harm or injury to come upon someone; a form of spiritual punishment, suffered in a physical manner. Right here we have exposed our identity, or cultural characteristics, as spiritual people.

Most Israelites, especially those born in the Caribbean or the Southern U.S.A., would understand about witchcraft, obeah or voodoo, although this is not what we are talking about. We are talking here about a very serious curse - slavery. So what have we done, and against whom did we do it, that we were sentenced to this terrible fate, and how do we end it? We should understand that the Christian Gentiles who enslaved us are spiritually inferior to us [Acts 15:6-10], so they could not have inflicted the curse on us. Then how could they have kept us in this state for almost 400 years? Even the Muslims who sold us to the Christian Gentiles are also spiritually weaker, Therefore, we are obviously dealing with another powerful spiritual force, one who has the ability to do anything He desires. To answer our first question then, with all our spiritual might, even today, only slavery could effectively bring us to our knees.

As Israelites, we should understand about the parting of the Red Sea; the plagues of Egypt; the parting of the River Jordan; the virgin birth; the conversion of water into wine and the resurrection of the dead. This is not to say that we know how to do these things, although in Haiti it is said that one could attend the funeral of a friend and three days after speak with him face to face in the market place. With all this power, Haiti is still the poorest country in the Western Hemisphere, so their power cannot be of truth and righteousness, but of evil - Deut. 18:10-12. Thus, the process of slavery, or the transformation of a nation of princes and princesses to cotton-pickers is very serious. Those who proudly worship the dead and the instrument of death, should also be seen as a highly spiritual enemy. It was against our Father, the King of the Israelites, The God of Abraham,The God of Isaac and The God of Jacob, that we have done wrong. Some people may ask, What kind of Father is this that would treat His children so badly? Do not forget that He is the same Father who first sent His son to show us how to live and to be sacrificed for our [Israelites] sins [Matt. 1:21-23; 2:6]. Secondly, we had a choice in this matter, which came with the deal [covenant] that we signed with our Father at Mt. Sinai - Ex. 24:3-8; Ex. 31:12-18; Lev. 26; Deut. 7; Deut. 11:26-28. We clearly selected the road we wanted to walk, which was contrary to the instructions of our Father. Now we only have ourselves to blame. Even with this knowledge today, only a few would attempt to make a change. Again, the choice is ours! Thirdly, this is not the first time that we have deliberately gone against the commands of our Father and were forgiven. We had several warnings, all of which we failed to heed. So what is our excuse?

If nothing else we must understand that whenever there is sin, there will be death. That was the law from the beginning [Gen. 2:16-17] and it cannot be changed. Death may be physical or spiritual, or both. We have all seen the living dead on our city streets, but there are also our living dead within Christian and Islamic institutions. Do not be fooled by their appearances, most times the dead look better than the living. We are all guilty of yielding to temptation, yet this is no excuse for not following the instructions as given by our Father. We should now understand that our consequences are by personal design; we should be very careful what we say and do from now on. We have a big responsibility for the well-being of our children, since they too will pay dearly for our mistakes and also their children in turn and so on. We are paying today for the errors of our ancestors, plus our own mistakes, This is the reason why ancestral worship [voodoo] is not only wrong, but also foolish; since it is simply a recycling of the errors of the past; tripling our burden. Instead, we should be looking to break that cycle of poverty, ignorance and death.

When we learn to appreciate the sacrifices that our Father made for us, the price that He paid to call us His own, then our enslavement would begin to make sense to us. Remember that there were no civilizations greater than Egypt and Ethiopia, yet they were both ransomed for us [Isaiah 43:1-4]. Now that is real love! Love based entirely on TRUTH! Our Father sent warning after warning, Prophet after Prophet and we ignored every warning and killed every Prophet. We lied and caused the death of our brother Jesus the Christ; persecuted his disciples and chased our brother Paul all over the Mediterranean trying to murder him.

Our Father is not at all unlike other fathers today, in some way. When our children disobey, what do we do as parents? Do we go next door and punish the neighbour's children? No! We punish our own and our God is no different - Amos 3:1-3. It is imperative, therefore, that we do not look at ourselves through the eyes of others, or even compare ourselves to others. Within our great book of instructions, the book of Judges lists six different records of our previous enslavement. 1) Judges 3:1-11, 8 years enslavement at the hand of the Babylonians. 2) Judges 3:12-15, 18 years enslavement at the hands of the Moabites. 3) Judges 4:1-3, 20 years enslavement at the hands of the Canaanites. 4) Judges 6:1-10, 7 years enslavement at the hands of the Midianites or Ishmaelites. 5) Judges 10:6-16, 18 years at the hands of the

Philistines and the Ammonites. 6) Judges 13:1-7, 40 years at the hands of the Philistines. After 930 B.C.E, when the kingdom of the Israelites was divided, the tribes of Judaea were enslaved for 70 years by the Babylonians - II Chron. 36-14-21. Surely after all this punitive action we should have learnt something.

There should be no more confusion about why we suffer today and why our lives are so hard. Someone had to pay for the disobedience of our forefathers [Ex. 20:1-6]; plus we also are guilty of the same crimes, which is even worse, since we possessed the transcripts of their activity. In order to remove the curse and break this cycle of spiritual poverty, we must assume our role of leadership, based on TRUTH and the truth is... we are Israelites, the children of the circumcision. We should read Solomon's prayer in the book of I Kings 8, especially verses 44-53. Then read the response of our Father in chapter 9:1-9. Our reason for being is to worship our King, The God of Abraham, The God of Isaac and The God of Jacob, in spirit and in truth and teach others, who seek the truth, to do the same.

This will in turn allow us to receive His gift of understanding, that we may be faithful like our forefather Abraham and obedient like our brother Moses. Only then will we inherit the wealth and power of the Promised Land. Only then would we ceased to be tossed to and fro by every man-made doctrine. Finally, we should be extremely thankful that we were only sentenced to 400 years of slavery, surely one can argue that we deserved much more. The good news is that it will soon end, but only for those who are prepared to adhere to the instructions of the Spirit of Truth - **THE COMFORTER**.

CHRISTMAS AND THE SLAVE

Christianity has **INTERPRETED** the Holy Scriptures according to its wild fancy, and has invented a "Christmas" where there is not even the most distant illusion to such a thing. The facts are:- there is no Christ in "Christianity"; Christianity is the worship of the sun or sun-god; Christianity or the Christian Empire received its doctrine from Babylon via Egypt and Rome; and Rome is the "Babylon" of Revelation chapter 17. We may also add that the Etruscans, who founded Rome around 575 B.C. emigrated from Babylon and settled in Northern Italy at Etruria or Tuscany.

According to Christianity, Jesus was born on December 25th. But according to the Holy Scriptures this is definitely not true, even to the slightest degree. In Luke 2:8-9, when the angel announced the birth of Jesus, shepherds were attending their flocks at night in an open field. This act of the shepherds would be practically impossible on December 25th due to the severe winter conditions and poor vegetation. Luke 2:1-5 indicates it was taxation time and citizens had to travel to the city to pay their taxes. Taxes were not collected during the winter, but rather during the fall.

Throughout the entire history of the Israelites there was no such festival as Christmas, but there was a pagan festival celebrated by heathens and Gentiles at the time of the winter solstice, from December 21st to December 25th. In Babylon, where this festival began, it commemorated the birth of Ninus or Nimrod, who was the son of Queen Semiramis or Rhea reincarnated, since Nimrod was her husband before his death. Semiramis was also worshipped as the "queen of heaven."

In Egypt, the exact application was made to Osiris, Isis and Horus. Horus being Osiris re-born. Osiris was buried on December 21st and Horus born on December 23rd. Note his "resurrection" being on the third day. Sounds familiar?

In Greece, Nimrod was called Bacchus, from whom we get "bacchanal;" [drunken revelry]. Bacchus was always identified with the **IVY** branch, which in turn identified him as the son [branch] of Khus or Cush [BacCHUS]. Now where did "Ivy League" come from, and what does it really mean? Well at least we know where the red berries on the ivy of the Christmas decorations originated, and what they mean.

In Rome, Nimrod was called Saturn and his festival was known as the Saturnalia. The Romans also worshipped the Persian sun-god Mithras. His festival, the Brumalia, was held at the same time, starting on December 22nd. The Brumalia was also known as "the Birthday of the Unconquered Sun".

Among the pagan Anglo-Saxons the sun was also worshipped and still is today. On December 21st, the winter solstice, or the shortest day of the year, they mourn the death of the sun-god. It is called "the Holly King". When the sun re-appears a few days later, it is called "the Oak King" and is worshipped with wine and cakes. This practise is part of the craft of **WICCA** or witchcraft. They too call on the "queen of heaven" and the "horned hunter or horned god"; i.e Semiramis and Nimrod. [Horns were a symbol of strength and power and Nimrod (Kronos) was so depicted]. So there it is - the **HOLLY**, the **OAK** and the **WREATH** (death).
Now December 25th was first called **"YULE DAY"** by the pagan Anglo-Saxons, even before Christianity. **"YULE"** is a Chaldean

name for "infant" or "little child"; hence "yule-cake" [Scotland] and "nur-cake" [France], or "birth-cake", or "birthday-cake". Also, the "yule log" is symbolic of the death of Nimrod. He, like Osiris, was "cut down" by his enemy at the height of his power. Osiris [sun-god] was killed by Typhon and shut up in a tomb of darkness [winter], then to rise again as Horus. However, in Babylon Nimrod was also depicted as a tree stump, hence the "yule log". But that old serpent, the symbol of life to the Babylonians and the Egyptians, wrapped itself around the tree stump [Nimrod], causing a young tree to sprout up on the side. Hence the re-birth of Nimrod, Tammuz, Osiris, Bacchus etc.

[Now reference Genesis 2:9 and the next time we see that so-called medical symbol, we should understand]. Thus the burning of the "yule log" is supposed to produce the "Christmas tree", which when decorated after being cut down, is given new life again. Note the celebration of death, with the next most important symbol at this time, after the Christmas tree, i.e. the wreath. This symbol of death as a representation of life is ridiculous. A wreath is a wreath, and it belongs to the Christian cemetery. What other proof do you need!

WHAT NAME SHOULD THE CHILDREN OF SLAVERY BE CALLED

Are we West Indians
Negroes, coloreds, blacks,
African-Americans or
African-Canadians?

In this article, we shall conclusively prove the Israelite identity of the descendants of slaves. We shall draw on verifiable historical facts, biblical proof, as well as cultural and spiritual evidence to explain their nationality. In this process, we shall clearly demonstrate that, contrary to popular belief, our ancestors were NOT indigenous to Western Africa, but migrated to that region from the land of Ancient Israel.

Of course, this point of view will automatically generate questions regarding the Gentiles (Khazars) who call themselves "Jews"; we shall also address this matter. It is an undeniable fact that none of the nicknames adopted by the Children of Slavery, as our identity, make any sense; there is no solid foundation, no roots from which we can build and prosper. How else do we explain our sad plight today? How many times have you heard the comment, "Man know thyself"? Yet the same people quoting such wisdom are foolishly trying to build a house, and a very big one at that, without first laying the foundation. It is an exercise in futility!

How long are we going to continue to be the laughing stock of the world? Much has been written on our West African sojourn and most of it very well indeed, but only a handful of writers have dared to go beyond West Africa in seeking the truth about our identity. We shall concentrate on breaking this new ground, but before you accuse me of disturbing the peace, just ask yourself why do our youths embrace Egypt and Ethiopia, instead of Ghana, Nigeria, or the Congo. Remember, just recently, according to one of our local newspapers, the Somali [Ethiopia] women were spurning our handsome black American soldiers, laughing at their big, flat, broad noses, when compared to the small, narrow noses of the Somali or Ethiopian. Only if they both knew that the power is in the nose and therefore the bigger, the better. It is quite clear, however, that despite our common black skin, there is a big difference among black people of the world. This is known by the Ethiopian [Egyptian included], but is not understood by us today and therefore not addressed.

Another good example, proving that all black people are not the same, may be seen in the present crisis of Rwanda. The underlying factor is racial, yet both major groups have beautiful black skin. The majority, the Hutu [85%] claim to be semitic, while the minority, Tutsi [14%] are Hamitic like the Ethiopian or Egyptian. Of course, many a so-called scholar would tell you that Hutu are a "Bantu" people, with a strong, stocky built and a big, broad nose. The Tutsi, on the other hand, are considered tall and handsome, with a small, narrow nose; some even say that they are caucasoid - whatever that means.

The truth is that it was a German Gentile, Mr. Wilhelm Heindrick Bleek [1827-1875], who invented the meaningless term "Bantu", which has successfully hidden the true Semitic identity of most of the population of Central and Western Africa. Therefore, was it a coincidence that around the same time that the word Bantu was invented, that the word Semitic took on a new and different meaning, even allowing for the introduction of the new word of

"Semitism"? How clever indeed! This Gentile deception was also responsible for the cover-up of the Israelite identity of our North African ancestors, by the invention of the word "Berber".

Without trying to put down anyone who is desperately seeking the truth, we must be sure to allow logic and common sense to rule at all times. What is being revealed here is not entirely new, but emotions and prejudices have suppressed the obvious. We are dealing strictly with knowledge of self. The proof is in the mirror, not between the pages of any text. The text should only serve to clarify and therefore to confirm what is already known. In fact, some of our parents and grandparents should be our text; question them before it is too late. Through their "old-fashioned" ways, we might be able to learn something about our true culture, that was and still is being taken for granted.

A LOOK AT OUR NAMES

Today, we refer to ourselves as "West Indians", "Negroes", "coloreds", "blacks", "Afro- Canadians", African Canadians", "African Americans", etc. Who are we really, as descendants of slaves? Are we Indians from the west? How did we arrive at these nicknames and then try to convert them into a national identity? Out of the navigational failure of Christopher Columbus came the title "West Indian". Around 1555, the Portuguese were the first to refer to black people by the term "Negro". Then along came the German Johann Friedrich Blumenbach [1752-1840], who was the first to attempt to change that three races of humanity into five. He superficially divided humanity by skin colour, allowing "the Negro" for the black component. The Latin version of Negro is "niger", also meaning black and from which we got "nigger". It is important to note that the foregoing people are European, the ones who have enslaved our foreparents and now are enslaving us mentally. Why are we still allowing this same European to decide our identity? Why not seek the truth for ourselves?

Surely, as educated people, we should have known that the word "Negro" is an adjective, thereby making it grammatically incorrect for us to call ourselves by that word. The same goes for "colored" and "black"; even "nigger", as a corruption of "niger", is wrong grammatically. However, we were so accustomed to following that we did not stop to investigate the accuracy of the given identity. What was even more humorous, [actually it was quite sad] was when we went from calling ourselves "Negro" to calling ourselves "black". We were a people who were definitely lost, grasping at straws in an ocean of confusion, not knowing how to swim. We did not know that Negro [Spanish/Portuguese] and black [English] meant the same thing.

Thus the deceivers of this world must have had a good laugh, while the sympathizers wept silently, as we proudly made fools of ourselves in ignorance. Looking back, we should now be able to see how we were set up to concentrate only on colour, our blackness, rather than look for cultural affiliation. So where does this leave us today as far as our identity is concerned? All other ethnic groups are known by the nation from which they came, and not by the colour of their skin. What is our national origin or nationality?

Have you even met an African? People from that continent usually introduce themselves very proudly as Ghanian, Nigerian, Ugandan, Egyptian, etc., specifying their tribe if necessary. The only people who constantly refer to themselves as Africans are the descendants of slaves, who are trying to be what they call "conscious". Such consciousness we could definitely do without, since it makes us look quite foolish. Such consciousness is generally used for ulterior motives, rather than to educate and uplift. Can we be a little more specific and explain from which nation in Africa? How about detailing a few tribal customs, especially their origins? If we really understood our history, we would have known that most of the cultural practices of Western Africa are perversions, albeit innocent, of a lost Israelite custom. This fact alone should spur our consciousness and we should seek further, rather than settling for what is popular and emotionally appealing. Africa is a land of diverse cultures, yet wherever the descendants of the slaves are found, that culture is fairly constant.

BEFORE WESTERN AFRICA

Within a year after the death of King Solomon around 930 B.C., the kingdom of the Israelite was divided by internal strife; to the north was Israel and to the south Judaea. This strife continued over the next 100 years causing many to flee their land (Israel). This weakness allowed the Assyrian king, Sargon II, to invade the Israelites in 722 B.C. In 597 B.C., the Babylonian king, Nebuchadnezzar II attacked, and again in 586 B.C. The Greek Selucid King Antiochus IV [Ephiphanes] invaded in 168 B.C. and the Roman Pompey in 63 B.C. Finally, in 70 A.D., the Roman General Titus put the last nail in the Israelite's coffin, when he destroyed the Temple at Jerusalem. By 135 A.D. practically all our Israelite ancestors were driven to seek refuge throughout the Mediterranean lands, especially Egypt and Northern Africa.

In Egypt, after establishing exclusive Israelite communities at Alexandria in the delta and Elephantine Island by the first cataract, they followed the course of the Nile southward to the Sudan, beyond Khartoum. At Kordofan, along the White Nile, the

Israelites travelled westward, although a few settled in Uganda. On the trek toward Lake Chad, they joined other brethren travelling from Arabia and Yemen, and thence on to the Western Sudan.

In North Africa, predominantly Israelite communities were to be found at Cyrenaica, Leptis Magna and the hinterland of Carthage, in rural Numidia and Mauritania [Algeria/Morocco]. Due to their refusal to worship the Roman Emperor, the Israelites were severely persecuted and were forced to flee across the Sahara Desert for safety. Even from Italy, Greece and Asia [Turkey] they poured into North Africa on their trek to Western Sudan, leaving the Romans to believe that they would perish in the desert sand.

What ever persecution the Romans forgot to inflict, the Mahommedans [Ishmaelites or Muslims] perpetuated against the Israelites. By 708 A.D. all North Africa was under Muslim control, as they executed their motto, "convert or die". Israelites who could not flee to Western Sudan, simply converted to Islam. One such Israelite was Tarik-ibn-Ziad, for whom the Rock of Gibraltar was named. In 711, as Governor of Mauritania, he led an invasion of mainly Israelites into Iberia [Spain/Portugal], defeating King Roderic in the process.

This Israelite conqueror was eventually defeated at the French Pyrenees. For the next 780 years, the Moors [Israelites and Muslims] ruled in Iberia; the Muslims dominating the political scene and the Israelites laying the foundation for European civilization. Between 900 and 1300 A.D., Spain became the most educationally advanced country in the world, as the Israelites led the field in science, astronomy, mathematics, finance, philosophy, mysticism, literature, religion, medicine and geography. All the nations of Europe came to Spain to drink of Israelite knowledge. The few "black" historians who touch on this subject, do so under the heading of Muslim or "black" history, without specifying our unique Israelite identity and culture. This is a classic example of our deplorable state of mental slavery.

Finally, in 1478, as the Europeans started to assert themselves and with the Muslim power structure weakening due to internal strife, the Spanish Inquisition was established. This Christian institution promoted the Christian philosophy at the expense of the Israelite culture. The "convert or die" slogan was now applied by the Christians; Israelites were forcefully deported to Northern or Western Africa. This is the part of history that others have purposely excluded, in order to ensure our mental enslavement and deception, by inventing a fictitious "Jew".

We must read "The Word The Israelites and The Damned", edited by Shadrock, to acquire a better understanding of this matter. A decree to expel all Jews [Israelites] was issued on March 31, 1492 by King Ferdinand and Queen Isabella of Spain. Many fled to Portugal, but there too the Christian government of King Manoel issued its decree expelling all Israelites in 1496. The only sanctuary for an Israelite was found in Western Sudan, none went to Europe. By then Columbus had sailed, using navigational charts and other equipment invented by Israelites and as they say, the rest is history.

THE KHAZARS

Many people may ask, "if the descendants of slavery are Israelites, then who is the white male that calls himself a Jew?" To be exact, he is the Gentile Khazar; the seventh son of Togarmah, who was Japheth's grandson and brother of Ashkenaz. According to our history book, in Genesis 10:2-5, his great uncle was Magog of Gog and Magog fame. This fact will come in handy later. From about 600 to 1000 A.D. this Khazarian formed Eastern Europe's largest and most powerful kingdom of approximately one million square miles, with its capital at Itil. Its southern border touched the Caucasus mountains and the Black Sea; on the east was the Caspian Sea or Sea of the Khazars and the Volga river; on the north, the Ural mountains; and to the west, Kiev and the Ukrainian Steppes. As a barbaric tribe speaking a Turkish language, the history of the Khazars go back to 200 A.D. where they existed as subjects to Attila the Hun. Thanks to the Khazars Europe was spared the Muslim onslaught, as they defeated the Arabs in 653 A.D. at Balanjar. The Khazars therefore held the balance of power between the Mahommedans and the Byzantine Christians.

Despite his efforts to cover up his true heritage as a pagan Gentile, which is essential if he is to deceive the world into thinking that he is really a Jew, the Khazarian, along with the help of the Christians, has inadvertently revealed much about his past. It is next to impossible for anyone to read a recent text book on European history and find anything at all on the Khazars. Why would such an important era in history of the proud European Gentile, who always go to great lengths to document their bravado, even lying, why would it be missing? Well, thank God for the conscience, some Khazarian authors have decided to tell the truth and so a few old books may still be available. This has left the Khazarian in a state of perpetual denial; but there are several methods to obtain the truth if you know how to investigate. However, let us deal with the so-called "Jewish" question.

As pagans, the Khazars practise, as they did from the beginning, a form of sorcery called "shamanism" and their priest was referred to, in their Yiddish dialect, as a Shammes. Already at the very root of their culture is the word "sham", meaning a cheap imitation. Never-the-less, their Khagan (king) Bulan invited representatives of Islam, Christianity and the Israelites to discuss their individual doctrines, in order to determine which was closest to the truth. Unanimous agreement was given to the doctrine of the Israelites, so about 740 A.D., the Khagan decided to convert his nation in an effort to imitate the ways of an Israelite. By this time the twelve tribes of the Israelites were long scattered among the heathens of this world, mainly to Africa, Asia and Iberia (Spain/Portugal) and had began to lose their religious purity. The Khazars then invited Pharisees (Israelites) from Babylonia to teach them from the Talmud. We must examine this era very carefully, in order to gain some perspective of the prevailing conditions at the time.

Between the 5th and 12th centuries, the best that the Gentile Europeans could offer at that time was called the Dark Ages. This was their period of little or no progress, massive illiteracy and backwardness. The only bright spot was within the walls of the Christian Institution and that knowledge was used mainly for evil rather than to illuminate the masses.

Of course, the Israelites in Spain flourished in isolation from the rest of Gentile Europe. Now just imagine an Israelite Pharisee, who was accustomed to producing spiritual documentations such as the Holy Bible, arriving in Khazaria, the very personification of Gentile savagery. It is now common knowledge that the Khazarians were forced to make changes to the "Babylonian Talmud" due to their lack of understanding. As a result, they produced their own perverted European version, just like their other pagan Gentile brethren, the Christians, who continue even to this day to produce corrupted versions of the Authorized English Translation of the Israelite scriptures, because they too lack understanding. What would the Khazars have done if the Pharisees had decided to teach them the real doctrine from the Holy Scriptures?

The Khazars, however, adopted certain basic physical Israelite customs, such as circumcision and worshipping their god on the Sabbath Day. Due to these practices, the Khazar has been affectionately nicknamed a "Jew" by pagan Mahommedans and the infidel Christians, who would not know a real Jew of the tribe of Judah from a Benjamite of the tribe of Benjamin. These are the same ridiculous people who called Mohammed a prophet and Paul a Christian; even though Jesus the Christ stated that John the Baptist was the last Prophet - Matt. 11:11-15 and Luke 16:15-17; and Paul identified himself as an Israelite - Rom. 11:1-3 and Phil. 3:5. No Israelite has ever and will never refer to a Khazarian as a "Jew". Ironically, the Khazars refer to themselves as Ashkenazim, reflecting their true heritage from the line of Japheth, since Ashkenaz was their uncle.

Thus the Khazars combined their practise of shamanism and their other pagan rituals, to help form their unique Gentile pagan culture of "Judaism", as a 16th century Eastern European product. This Khazarian cult of Judaism has nothing to do with the bible and was unknown by our Israelite forefathers. After Khazaria was absorbed into Russia during the 11th century, many Khazarian became citizens of Eastern European countries and some later migrated to Western Europe. This brought them in contact with a few of the Israelites of Spain (Sephardim). Since the Khazars were light years behind the Sephardims in every sense and therefore had nothing in common, they were forced to isolate themselves until the expulsion of the Israelites to Western Africa,

when they assumed the role of impostor to this day.
The irony of this whole matter is seen when some of the Children of Slavery, while seeking their roots, somehow get themselves confused with the Khazars and Judaism. As a matter of fact, the Khazars have taught, or are teaching Israelites in the U.S.A. and the Caribbean. How is it possible that they have tried to learn from us and failed, but now are teaching us? What can they teach us? Yiddish is not Hebrew and never will be. As Israelites, we do not have to speak Hebrew because our scriptures have been quite accurately translated into English. This is simply common sense. What else is there to say?

There is not a single human being on this planet who could point out what is incorrect with the substance of the Authorized Translation. Plus the ancient Hebrew language has not been spoken or ever written since the 6th century B.C. At that time the Israelites returned from Babylonia speaking mainly Aramaic, which was very close to Hebrew. Those trying to speak Hebrew today clearly demonstrate their lack of understanding of the scriptures; hence they try to impress others, or cover up their ignorance. Many variations to the ancient Hebrew have been written and spoken, mainly academically, but those are only imitations and can never be accurately classified as the real language.

THE SLAVE TRADE

By 790 A.D. the splendour of the Israelite Empire of Ghana was known world-wide. Ghana was called "The Land of Gold" and there was not a wealthier Empire anywhere to be found. Soon another form of gold would be available for trade. That special Israelite gold, which reflected both the wisdom and wrath of our God, was also indicative of a people filled with the spirit of disobedience. As Israelites, we should all remember the year 1076, the year in which the first of two forces of evil were unleashed on Western Africa. The Mahommedans, or Muslim sect called the Almoravids, attacked with devastating results. It must be stressed that these Muslims were black people, differing mainly in appearance from the Israelites by the earrings and turban they wore. They ruthlessly imposed their Islamic cult on the Israelite elite, ravaged the Empire and imposed heavy taxes. Western Africa would never be the same again. Attempts to rebuild were quite successful in Mali and Songhai, but the evil presence of the Mahommedans refused to go away. In 1591, they attacked again and the lights over Western Africa went out permanently. Now it was time to unleash the second force of evil.

The second force of evil was easily found in the white Gentile Christians. Armed with the blessings of their Pope, the deadly cross and the sword, they arrived deceptively on the Western Coast of Africa as traders and missionaries in the 15th century. With the combined forces of evil, as manifested by Mahommedans and Gentile Christians, the punishment of the Israelites for their transgressions against the laws of their God was about to begin. Thus the stage was set for the trading of over fifty million Israelites, between black Mahommedans, who sold us and white Gentile Christians, who bought us.

This manifestation of evil forces by the hands of Islam and Christianity was the greatest crime ever perpetrated against humanity. It is very important to observe then that the problem facing the Children of Slavery is of a spiritual nature and not one of colour. Physical applications however good they may be, are totally useless when seeking the solution. Let us examine this point of spirituality further.
First of all, we must reference our spiritual text to understand the

prophecies as follows: 1) Gen. 15:13 regarding our 400 years of enslavement. It is important to note that although the Israelites spent 430 years in Egypt, only about half of that time were they enslaved; they actually ruled Egypt, forming the XVth and XVIth Dynasties. 2) Gen. 16:11-12 regarding the evil of the Muslims; 3) Lev. 26:14-45 regarding the punishment for our disobedience (slavery); 4) Deut. 28:15-68 regarding our punishment and enslavement; and 5) Rev. 17 and 18 regarding the Great Whore, which is Christianity or the wife of Lucifer. Note that this Mother of harlots is the abomination of the earth, and will be drunk with the blood of the Saints and the Prophets who are Israelites. Finally, to tie this whole package together, the mysteries of Christianity are hidden in Freemasonry, which is dominated by the Khazars. As we can see, our enemies are also applying the principles of their spirituality, which is good in a way because this is our strongest suite. Therefore, if we play our cards correctly, we can win; although it will not be easy.

"NEGRO SPIRITUALS"

Throughout all the land of the Americas, the Israelites sang certain folk songs during their enslavement. Due to the nature of these songs, they were called "spirituals" because they came from deep within, from the spirit. Without getting too deep, let us just say that the slaves were not physically controlling their singing. In fact, they probably did not fully comprehend everything they sang about, but such is the power of the spirit. This point is important since it indicates a state of much innocence and objectivity and therefore may be used to accurately assess the identity of the slaves. Furthermore, folk songs have a tremendous impact on the culture of any nation. They are part of the folklore of a nation, the very essence from which the cultural fabric is woven. These songs represent a nation's beliefs, customs, history, proverbs or narratives, literature, art and crafts, etc. Every nation has its unique folklore and the slaves were no different. If the slaves had originated from Egypt, they would have to sing about Osiris, Isis, the Pyramids, the Nile, the Sphinx and the power of the Pharaohs. If they were Muslims or Ishmaelite slaves, they would sing about Allah, Mohammed, the Koran, the Kaaba, the black stone or Mecca. If they were British slaves, they would sing about the Thames, the Scots, the Picts, the Druids, the Romans and the Anglo-Saxons. If the slaves originated in West African, they would have to sing about the Sahara, the Niger, the Congo, Timbuktu, the oasis, the salt mines and the gold mines. The point is that when led by the spirit, a person can only produce what is natural or indigenous to that spirit. Now what did the slaves sing about?

The slaves of the Americas sang about Moses and the Exodus; Pharaoh's drowning in the Red Sea; the Promised Land; the River Jordan; Joshua's tumbling of the walls of Jericho; the Hebrew Children and their ole time religion; Jacob's ladder; Ezekiel's vision of the wheel (Cherubim); Daniel's vision of the stone made without hands; Daniel in the lion's den; Nebuchadnezzar and the hand writing on the wall; their enslavement in Babylon; the Sabbaths and Zion. Notice that there was NOTHING sung about Christmas, Easter, Good Friday, or Ramadan.

Therefore, we can safely say that the foregoing facts clearly indicate an Israelite cultural identity. In addition, at that time the slaves, who could not read nor write, were taught on Sunday morning from the New Testament by their Gentile Christian master. What else could he teach? There is no place in the Old Testament where he could find himself, so he had to go to the books of Paul. Yet just about everything sung by the Israelite slaves, who were not allowed to read or write, even if they could,was from the Old Testament. So what if our culture is only found between the pages of the Holy Bible? We have no control over these facts and should be proud to proclaim our cultural heritage. The Israelite Scriptures were written by us, exclusively for us and about us; and were not intended for world-wide circulation. We might as well get use to these facts, because they cannot be changes, neither can they be erased by anyone. Thus, the mystery of the "Negro Spirituals" is no more. This is just another proof that the Children of Slavery are Israelites and should only refer to themselves as Israelites.

JUDAISM! A WORD CREATED

The word "Judaism" is wrongfully and carelessly used today to describe the religious practices or culture of the Ancient Israelites. Unfortunately, many believe that "Judaism" was derived from "Judah or Jews", but nothing could be further from the truth. **There is no historical or factual record anywhere that may be accurately used to make such a case.** In fact, let me respectfully challenge any Khazarian or Yiddish to produce such evidence. How come the word "Judaism" only became known in the 18th century? **There was not one single Israelite who knew anything about Judaism. Furthermore, the Holy Bible, the sacred book of the Israelites, does not mention the word "Judaism".**

Thus, this man-made name that turned into a philosophy, has nothing to do with the God written about in the Holy Scriptures. According to the teachings of the bible, the choice must be made between the God of the Israelites or Lucifer. To go against one is to serve the other; so to ignore the instructions of the bible is to worship Lucifer. We shall examine the major pillars of Judaism in order to determine the nature of this philosophy and also to see on which side it falls.

The evolution of Judaism is equated with the rise to world prominence among the descendants of the Khazars, who were an Eastern European pagan tribe. Although the Khazars lost their kingdom [Khazaria] mainly to the Russians between the 11th and 12th centuries, they found it easy to maintain their unique tradition through a common dialect called Yiddish. **This makes Judaism a tradition that is specifically of European origin.** Today the Khazars or Yiddish are affectionately called "Jews", a nickname which, since the expulsion of the Israelites or "Negroes" from Spain and Portugal between 1492 and 1498, has served their purpose. It is important to notice the impact of a nickname, theirs and ours, but we all know that a nickname is no substitute for accurate identity. There has to be a greater substance involved, something that is beyond the physical; there must be the spirit. **These East European Gentiles do not share the same, or even similar cultural traits as the Ancient Israelites and therefore have nothing in common with the Jews from the tribe of Judah.** Is it at all conceivable that a nation could have changed its cultural values and characteristics so drastically?

Why would the Khazars want to separate themselves from the fountain-head of Western civilization? What is even more confusing is that the Khazar steadfastly lays claim to the heritage of the Ancient Israelites; yet knows absolutely nothing about their culture, especially their religion. To find such cultural traits we have to look among the Children of Slavery throughout the Americas. Thus by comparing the practices of the Khazars with the doctrine or culture of the Israelites, we shall prove conclusively that the so-called Jew is only a Gentile and therefore pagan.

Every Friday night the Khazarian family which practices Judaism performs a voodoo-like ritual at sunset. In such a Khazarian family room there are lighted candles, wine, food and flowers. Then a circle is formed around the candles while the Khazars sing and pray. All that is missing are the drums and the dancing to claim the voodoo rites, but then again even the rhythm would be strange to them seeing that they are accustomed to their cantor.
The family consumes the wine and food in a party atmosphere.

This ritual apparently culminates in sexual intercourse in an attempt to express the union between the God of the Israelites [Bridegroom] and His chosen people [Bride]. This is supposed to be the beginning of the Israelite Sabbath, but since the Khazars are not Israelites, they therefore pervert His instructions through their ignorance.

When we examine the doctrine of the Israelites, we find that there is no precedence in the Torah for drinking wine or strong drink on the Sabbath. In fact the God of the Torah strictly forbids the use of wine, grapes and strong drink, by Israelites, while serving Him - Lev. 10:8-11; Num. 6:1-4; Isa. 28:7-8; Ezek. 44:21; and Luke 1:13-16. In Lev. 15:16-18 it also proves that sexual activity on the Sabbath is contrary to the instructions of our God. But this fact only applies to Israelites and not to the Khazars. We should understand that our God has nothing against sex, but since the pagans have always indulged in sexual activities as part of the worshipping of their gods, even enticing some Israelites to do the same in Samaria, it is good for us to distinguish ourselves. After such intercourse, the couple must bathe and would be considered unclean until the evening, as far as contact with holy things are concerned.

The Sabbath is a holy day and thus contact with the holy things of our God would be inevitable, hence abstinence is necessary. Why would the Khazars, who falsely lay claim to the Torah [the first five books of Moses] deliberately go against its instructions? Could it be that the culture of the Torah is foreign to the Khazar? His behaviour is therefore a display of ignorance.
On December 25th the Khazars celebrate "Hanukkah", a Christmas-style eight-day party. The only difference between Hanukkah and Christmas is the lighting of their eight-branched

Khazarian candlestick. The God of the Torah gave no such instructions for either "Hanukkah" or an eight branched candlestick. The candlestick used by the Israelites to worship their God has three branches on each side, for total of seven.

There is no such thing as an eight or nine-branched menorah. From whom then came these blasphemous instructions? How could the Khazar make such a gigantic blunder with an item of such importance as the candlestick and still call himself a Jew? The Torah is quite explicit and the Khazarian is supposed to be very smart, but the higher a monkey climbs, the more it reveals under its tail. In Ex. 25:31-40 the God of the Israelites gave us specific instructions on how to make our SEVEN-BRANCHED candlestick. This was confirmed in Ex. 37:17-24; Zech. 4:1-2; Rev. 1:12,20 and 4:5. From these facts we have clear evidence on which side of the coin Judaism falls.

In 148 B.C. after our Israelite brethren, the Maccabees, had defeated Antiochus and returned law and order to Judaea, they purged the Temple, built a new altar just like the previous one and dedicated it to our God on the 25th day of Casleu or Kislev (November/December). The previous altar was defiled by Antiochus, a Greek, who maliciously sacrificed swine's flesh in an effort to defeat the Israelites. At the new altar the Israelites offered up sacrifices, burnt offerings and praises to our God in an eight-day victory celebration. Led by Judas, called Maccabeus, the Israelites decided to ordain the dedication of the altar as a local annual even during their time. It was not a command from our God and besides, the entire Temple was since destroyed by the Roman Titus in 70 A.D. From this verifiable historical account the vast difference between the practises of the Khazars or Yiddish and the Israelites is quite obvious. **Everything was done exactly according to our law given by the hand of Moses from our God. Therefore, they had to use a** candlestick with **SEVEN BRANCHES** in order to conform to the law and to worship our God in spirit and in truth. Anything else would have been a mockery and extremely dangerous to us.

More confusion lies in the seventh month of Tishri (September/October) whereby "Rosh Hashanah" is celebrated; followed by "Kol Nidre"; then there is "Yom Kippur" and finally "Sukkot" is observed. [**The "Kol Nidre" is a Yiddish prayer which invalidates all vows, oaths, confessions, etc. for one year; it has no biblical foundation.**] The Khazars say that this season is associated with the creation of the world, but where is the proof! Why is there so much emphasis placed on death or the worshipping of the dead? If this were the time of creation, it would indeed be surrounded with life, since birth is the symbol of the beginning and death is the symbol of the end. During this season many Khazars reflect on the dead with visits to the grave site.

There is a memorial service or "yizkor" on the day of "Yom Kippur" in honour of the dead. In fact, the Khazars are proud to make public video documentation of their Shammes worshipping their god in the middle of their cemetery. Many Israelite martyrs who were killed by the Romans are honoured by the Khazars at this time and of course the sad stories of the holocaust are recited. But why would the Khazar, a descendant of Gog and Magog the enemy of the Israelites, want to honour Israelite martyrs? This makes absolutely no sense at all. Some Khazarians make pledges and donations or "tzedakah" in memory of the dead; while others light memorial candles and some visit the sick and the dying at the various infirmaries. This is also the time when the Khazar prepares his will, which seems like a very good idea since there is so much death in the air. Are all these practices of God?

Now when we compare this Khazarian depressing period of

darkness with the practices of the Israelites, the Yiddish look so stupid, it makes one wonder if they are desperately trying to appear to be what they are not. **Where are the biblical instructions to assign new names or new days to our God's holy days? We all have this tendency to want to be little gods, first changing names and seasons and then who knows what.** Of what language is "Rosh Hashanah" and "Yom Kippur"? Is it Hebrew, Aramaic or Yiddish? It must be made extremely clear that Hebrew and Aramaic are both different from Yiddish. Yiddish, which also refers to the Khazarian national, is a predominantly German dialect mixed with a Turkish language. The authorized version of the Israelite scriptures is written in English, which is also the language of the Israelites today. Thus, it would be wrong and foolish for an Israelite to assign a new name to our holy day and especially by using this foreign European dialect of Yiddish. Plus, we could not guarantee an accurate pronunciation anyway, which would be important, since the meaning of a word could change if expressed incorrectly.

Furthermore, the Israelite new year is not in the fall, but rather in the spring. This make more sense since spring-time represents a new beginning, while the fall is the time to harvest. Read Ex. 12:1-2; then Ex. 13:3-4 and Deut. 16:1. According to the Torah and the bible all these scriptures confirm 1) that Abib [March/April] is the first month of the Israelite calendar; 2) that the Exodus occurred on the first day of Abib and 3) that any other new year, by whatever name or date is of a pagan origin. Lev. 16:29-34 indicates the Day of Atonement should be observed on the tenth day of the seventh month. Lev. 23:23-32 and Num. 29:7 confirm this law and show that the new year and the Day of Atonement are SEVEN MONTHS apart, according to Israelite culture. But even if the Khazar happens to observe the Day of

Atonement, his "Kol Nidre" would nullify any effectiveness. In fact it would make a mockery of our God. Finally, the Feast of Tabernacles is observed on the fifteenth day of the seventh month - Lev. 23: 33-44; Num. 29:12 and Deut. 16:13-15.

It is quite obvious that the seventh month of Tishri is a very holy month to an Israelite. Therefore, dealings with the dead are generally avoided, a clear indication that we worship the God of the living and not the god of the dead [Lucifer]. Matt. 22:31-32 and Mark 12:26-27 prove that the God of the Israelite is the God of the living. Num. 19:11-22; Matt. 23:27 and Mark 5:1-13 prove that the dead is unclean. Now according to their customs, who are the Khazars worshipping? How do they justify their habit of paying homage to the dead? Where in the Torah or the Old Testament is it written that we should keep services in honour of the dead, especially on the Day of Atonement? This is a very serious matter that calls into question the Khazarian level of understanding of Israelite culture. It also proves that "Judaism" and "Judah" have nothing in common whatsoever.

The Khazarian ritual called "Passover" is another form of deception as a part of Judaism which should not be confused with the original Passover of the Israelites. Based on their practices, theirs is simply just another family social event, whereas ours is a highly spiritual occasion. To the Khazar the most important part of this event is the "Seder", which is a sort of discussion-feast. This ritual is based on the symposium of the Greeks and Romans. Subjects range from politics to art and are read from a specific book called a "haggadah". This is not lively spontaneous discussion, but the following of a prepared text. During the process of the Khazarian Passover four or five cups of wine are consumed, including one for someone they call "Elijah". It is good for the Khazar to drink the wine because the Israelite Elijah would not be able to eat any grapes, furthermore drink any wine, kosher or not, and definitely not on our Passover. When we read Ex. 12:1-17 and Ex. 13:3-10, regarding the instructions from our God on keeping our Passover, there is absolutely no comparison whatsoever.

It is extremely important that we, the children of slavery, do not allow others to teach us their folly. We should not follow after the Yiddish language, the custom of Judaism or the god of the Khazar. Neither should we want to dictate to the Khazars regarding their behaviour, since it has served them well. However, in the interest of our education, we have proven that 1) what the Yiddish are doing through Judaism is not of truth and is therefore contrary to the instructions from our God; 2) what is good for them would be tragic for us, since we have been separated through a different God - The God of Abraham, The God of Isaac and The God of Jacob; and 3) as long as they concentrate on following their European version of the Talmud, we will respect them. But when they try to use our book, the Holy Bible, for teaching, or even refer to themselves as Jews, we will vigorously defend our honour. We shall use the TRUTH, which is our sword, to expose and defeat them, then the world will know who is real and who is fake.

THE FINAL CURTAIN

In this book, we have proven conclusively the Israelite identity of the descendants of slaves living in the Americas - God's chosen people. We have also proven that as Israelites our problem is spiritual in nature and not physical. Therefore, our solution must also be spiritual. It should be quite obvious that it is no coincidence that our strength lies in our spirituality. Common sense dictates that we begin from a position of strength; but we have clearly demonstrated that the spirituality of Christianity, Islam, Judaism, Voodoo, New Age, etc. would be wrong for us. Subsequently, we should understand why all the good physical efforts, like politics, social programmes and economics, as well as other spiritual alternatives, have all failed and will continue to fail. Such attempts at solving our problem can only address the symptoms and not the root cause. What is most interesting is that others have been able to make such physical efforts work quite effectively for themselves. It is therefore imperative that we as Israelites comprehend and appreciate our spiritual difference. From this point on we must distinguish ourselves by this behaviour, leading by example instead of following.

We have now reached the restricted zone and each reader must make a personal decision. Only those who have resolved to leave Egypt [slavery] and cross the Red Sea can make the trek to the Promised Land [Liberty]. The journey will be long and difficult, even dangerous, so we must be in one accord. We cannot afford to take any chances, so tourists and skeptics are not allowed, even beautiful black skin is not enough. From now on TRUTH is all that matters and only those sharing the same willingness to understand [philosophy, identity, mission, etc.] will be considered brethren, ALL others will be excluded concerning our spiritual matters. Needless to say, this idea makes more sense than just calling every and anyone brother or sister, simply because of the colour of his or her skin.

Family should always be united, sharing and loving each other. Thus who is not with us, is against us. Regardless of what we do, we must be honest with ourselves. No one will hold a gun to our head, or make us feel guilty and there is nothing to be converted to. But each person is responsible for his or her own soul, so laying blame is a waste of time. This trek will become more complex as we approach the Promised Land, therefore a good basic understanding is essential. There will be much to learn and it will always be based on what was understood before. This may be a good time for a review before embarking on the Path to the Promised Land.

As stated earlier, the driving force behind our solution will be **TRUTH**. We must be governed by the Spirit of Truth at all times, who is the Spirit of God or the Comforter. He is our only leader, the one and only Father, Reverend or Rabbi. Our aim should be to conduct ourselves with moral excellence, having a clear understanding of personal accountability. Living among the heathen has kept us in darkness. As Israelites, we must first seek knowledge of self, which is readily available from the scriptures, our historical record and instruction manual, in order to be illuminated and strengthened. We should not be distracted by others who maliciously and foolishly pretend to use our culture for their so-called religious rituals. Our forefathers documented their history, culture and philosophy for our benefit, as their descendants. With this knowledge of self, we should conclude that if our disobedience to our God caused us to be cursed, dispersed and enslaved, then obedience and fear of His judgment should bring us back under His wings. Thus led by the Spirit of Truth and armed with knowledge of our true identity and the gift of understanding, we should take our staff and head straight for

the shores of the new spiritual birth and never look back.
Arriving on the shore we will find other Israelites waiting to make their exodus from Egypt [mental slavery]. For the first time since the days of King Solomon we shall find ourselves in one accord under one God - one king, one doctrine, one philosophy, one identity and now one mission.

The doctrine of our forefathers, [scriptures] will be our bond. These scriptures shall be our instruction manual for a successful life and should help us to accept our full responsibility as world leaders, teaching moral excellence to all those who seek it out. This is our mandate - to be a beacon unto all humanity, to be the salt of the earth, a Royal Priesthood teaching ALL PEOPLES about our God and leading them along the path of Truth. Unknowingly the citizens of this world are waiting, they seek the light, but behold darkness and are given salt without savour. Their teaching priests lay in the gutter, drunk with the wine of damnation. Others continue to rot in the valley of dry bones, or perish in the depths of despair. But the time appointed is close at hand and The Ancient of Days is stirring from His rest. Arise O Israel, assume your rightful place in this society, accept your responsibility and lead; together we should make a difference.

When we have crossed over, we must once again review our progress. Each individual must personally decide to be governed by TRUTH. This act alone will invoke the gift from the Spirit of Understanding. The individual is then guided to knowledge of self, which affirms his or her true identity. Further guidance is provided as the individual is led to seek out other like-minded persons, who share the same philosophy of truth. With a common ideology and identity, unity is not only easy, it is practically guaranteed. Only then will all the by-products of unity be realized;

e.g. respect, trust, love, peace and growth. As our gift of understanding increases, our mission statement begins to unfold. Each person continues to develop, assuming full responsibility for self and conducts his or herself as if he or she were the leader of the community. This process is called "**Leadership by Example**" and is the only form of leadership that is acceptable. Just imagine a nation of such individuals! Jail houses will be converted into school houses or closed, left in ruins as a testimony to the truth.

The dreaded police department would be reduced to a mere skeleton of good and effective civil servants; criminal lawyers will be unemployed; the economy could suffer and the stock market could tumble. In other words, the system built on lies could collapse. All this because of a little truth!

The process of leadership continues as the individual learns discipline, patience, justice, self-reliance and above all, humility, as he or she strives to attain the highest level of service to God. This status is only applicable when serving our God and our brethren. This is a good indicator of one possessing wisdom and understanding. With these vital components, the discipline of self-reliance and the dignity of self-confidence will be manifested. Only then will we be fully qualified to tackle the important issue of economics. Since as Israelites, we must trust and respect each other, it should be very easy for us to pool our resources in order to attain a strong and dynamic economic base. This in turn will allow our dollars to circulate longer within our Israelite economy and even attract external dollars for additional economic growth. As long as we stay on the path of Truth and be patient, our dividends will be great. This format is not at all too different from the present system, where the best dividends are generally realized over the longer term. But it should be made extremely clear that patience is not passivism, but confidence in self and in the chosen path of Truth. When we develop the mentality of being job creators rather than being job seekers, then we will learn how to build a sustainable economy. The bottom line is that we would be in firm control and all economic activity will be in accordance with our philosophy and cultural values. Participation should be open to all, but only on our terms. However, we must first demonstrate leadership and confidence.

Some may think that what we are proposing is too good to be realistic. Others may say that it is just too difficult. Well consider this:- we all know what is meant by the phrase, "Easy comes, easy goes", so let me be the first to tell you that this process is not going to be easy and that is what makes it so exciting. If it were easy everybody would be doing it, especially the rich people. If it were easy we would tend to take everything for granted and the whole matter would become pointless. It is an opportunity to go where no one has gone before, at least in modern times; to distinguish ourselves by being different and by being right at the same time; to achieve what many have wished for, but only a few will ever attain.

IT IS THE ONLY WAY TO LIBERTY, real freedom; even death will be defeated. If nothing else, it is truly worth the effort. Also, do not forget that in the days of our forefathers David and Solomon, we achieved unity, respect and love for each other and even economic and military power, so it is possible. But it all came through our spiritual strength - Israelite spirituality. What makes this process of liberty so hard is the simple fact that everything revolves around the individual. If it were a mass movement, with people waving placards and shouting slogans with clinched fists, we would need our own planet to accommodate everybody. However, all that is required is the body, soul and spirit and silence. Now think and decide. Should you require additional information, the channels of communication are open, but unless activated shall remain silent. Peace, Love and Truth!

A CHRISTIAN INSTITUTION:

Another form of pagan power. A spiritual prison for the children of slavery. The top is shaped like the hood of the KKK or a pyramid. The entrance at the doorway is in the shape of the triangle. The altar is of the dead; the evil powers of the old Egypt which enslaved the children of Israel, are still enslaving them now. There is much more to all this, that the natural ignorant eye cannot see.

CHRISTIAN CHURCH OR GOVERNMENT BUILDING?
This picture tells you how hard it is sometimes to tell the difference between church and state.

THE TRUE SYMBOL OF FREEMASONRY:
This picture reveals a man's face in Egyptian style headgear. This face is also part of a lion's body and on top of the lion's body, are rows of serpents. Another mark of the beast.
This time it is much clearer. The beast is really the representation of men. The men that honour the beasts. The agents of Lucifer.

ANOTHER PLACE OF WORSHIP

This looks to me like a place of worship, but I am not sure what is being worshipped here. We see what seems to be the rays of the sun, and on both sides the evergreen tree.(see the Tree in Egypt).

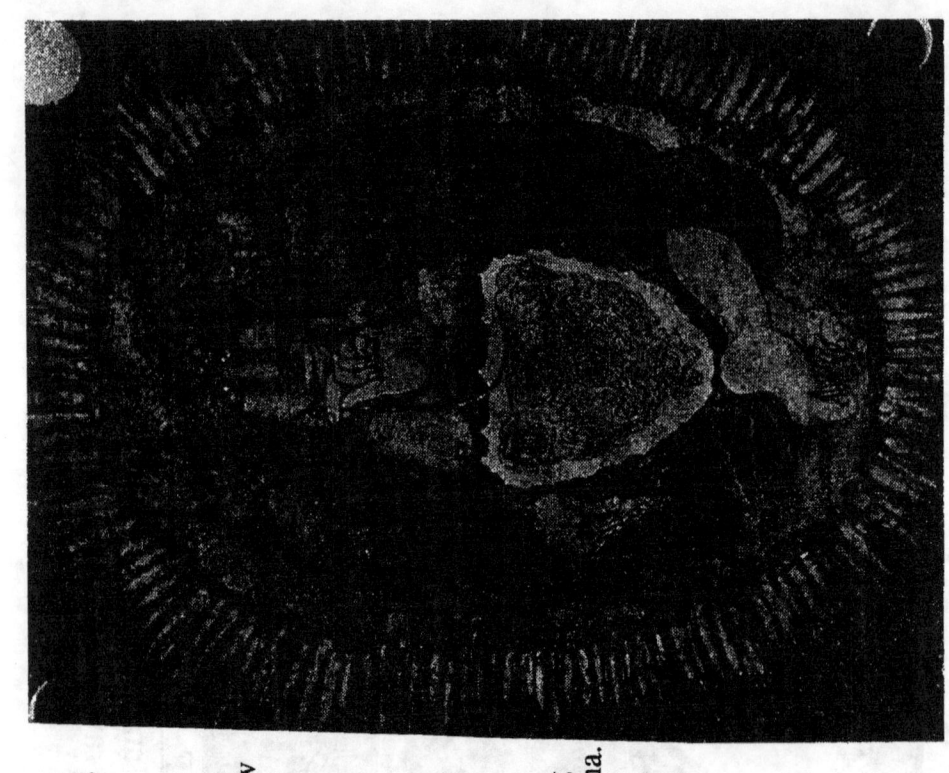

ON THE LEFT
An original Egyptian Obelisk at St. Peter's Rome: from 14 BC. This object that was once the symbol of power in Egypt, the enemy of God is now the power of the Western Society.
ON THE RIGHT
Hagia Sophia: This crafty painting is yet another Christian deception. When examined very carefully it is nothing but a woman's vagina. Those who have eyes let them see.

THE WASHINGTON MONUMENT:
This monument is a representation of the strength and power that America needed. It also represents the Egyptian god of fertility; **the erected Penis.** They took from the Egyptians the original obelisk and placed it in New York. But by their seat of Power they ignorantly fulfilled the scriptures, by building their own: identifying themselves as the new Egypt written about in the Bible. The Egypt that will suppress the children of Israel again. The Egypt where they would be sold for bondmen and bond women. Deuteronomy 28: 68. So they hewned their own stone, and built the image sealed in blood as the sacrifice to their gods; while we break our God's law. Exodus 20:25.

ANOTHER OBELISK:

It is said by some historians that this Obelisk was built in 1285 BC. Others said around 15BC. But one thing they all agreed on, that it was erected in 1836 at The Place de la Concorde in Paris

A CHRISTIAN CHURCH IN POTSDAM GERMANY.
This is living proof of deep rooted worshipping of the dead the Egyptian way, by honouring the organs of reproduction, Sun-worshipping, and Paganism. A Christian is a Christian any way you look at it, and this is the background of Christianity. In this picture "There is a Condom placed on the so-called church Obelisk above to mark aids awareness day December 1st. 1994. Its like putting it to the right and proper use

LADY OF GUADALUPE:
A Roman Catholic symbol of their Queen of heaven. Jer. 44: 17-30 **another vagina in disguise.** an abomination to the children of Israel. This is a great deception simply because it gives other Christians the opportunity to point the finger, hereby taking the guilt off themselves. But they all came out of her; the Great Whore.
They have learnt everything from her. She was the first to spread this pagan philosophy. So all are like unto her. From the so-called Baptist to the Evangelist.

A CHRISTIAN CEMETERY: Note the location of their so-called church.

This so-called church is in the midst of the dead. Could it therefore be of God? The children of slavery should be looking more carefully at this abomination. The symbol of death is the symbol of Lucifer, the prime cause of our sufferings. Come out of her my people. Come out of Christianity the GREAT WHORE. Revelation 18: 4.

A CHRISTIAN CEMETERY
Note the Obelisks. This symbol can be seen everywhere.
In the seat of power (Parliament), war memorials etc.
and of course the cemetery. The close relationship with
the dead plays a vital role in the recycling of familiar spirits
the symbol of their strength..

The Mark of the Beast: is not your credit card as you were told by your Christian teacher. It is Christianity itself. Notice in this picture taken in Washington DC. the serpent. Around this area is also a Christian Cemetery. We have decided not to put the picture of the serpent wrapped around the cross, because you can see that every day in the week on ambulances, and medical buildings.

FOR MORE INFORMATION ON THIS
VERY IMPORTANT SUBJECT ON

THE BIBLE AND THE BLACKMAN

CONCERNING THE CHILDREN OF SLAVERY

You must also read
READ

THE TRUTH THE LIE AND THE BIBLE

THE FORGOTTEN ISRAELITES

**THE WORD THE ISRAELITES
AND THE DAMNED**

Written by Shadrock

Tony Castrilli
Biblical Explanation of The Spirit

THE MOUNTAIN AND THE PIT

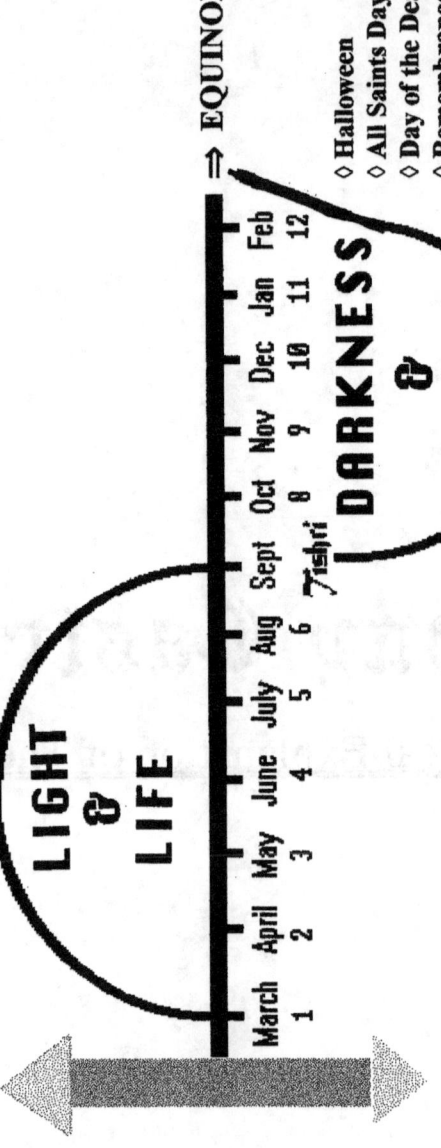

ZION
(June 21-25 ... Longest Day)

LIGHT & LIFE

⇒ EQUINOX

DARKNESS & DEATH

(Dec. 21-25 ... Shortest Day)
PIT

March 1, April 2, May 3, June 4, July 5, Aug 6, Sept 7 (Tishri), Oct 8, Nov 9, Dec 10, Jan 11, Feb 12

- ◊ Halloween
- ◊ All Saints Day
- ◊ Day of the Dead
- ◊ Remembrance Day
- ◊ Thanksgiving Day
- ◊ Christmas
- ◊ Kwanza
- ◊ New Year
- ◊ Carnival
- ◊ Lent Easter
- ◊ Valentine Day

* ABIB - New Year
* Spring
* Passover
* Day of Pentecost
* Baptism
* Marriage
* Blowing of trumpets
* Day of Atonement
* Feast of the Tabernacle

12 Hour Day
ABIB Begins>
12 Hour Night

In this part of the book we will discover concrete Biblical proof how the lie had dominated our society from the very core, so that every thing that springs from it, must adjust to its ways and pattern of life, and the living of it. I remember the words written in Romans the eleventh chapter and what it says especially from verses 13-21.

After reading this scripture we must understand what it is saying. We must be able to see that God has chosen Israel, and without the doctrine of Israel, the Gentiles cannot be saved. The teacher of the doctrine of truth must at all times be an Israelite or must be taught by an Israelite who knows, because it was the Israelite who was given the law and the promise, and the covenant, and Christ did not come for the world, but for the children of Israel and through them the Gentiles and heathens can be saved and not the way it is been taught today. Almost every religious programme on radio and television is owned, controlled and operated by Gentiles and a few children of slavery who don't know better, but are the faithful servants and students of the Gentiles, hereby making it very difficult for the truth to be told to the people that need it most, the Israelites. Romans 9:1-5.

Reflecting on all that you have just read, and I hope that you do understand, for the Bible is indeed a book of mystery, seeing that so simple scriptures can be manipulated in the minds of the ignorant for them to believe so strongly in the pagan philosophy known today as Christianity. It is so difficult for some people to see the evil of a philosophy that speaks of love more often than it is written in the Bible. Just in case you do not read the New Testament try reading Isaiah 11:9-10. Also Isaiah 42:5-6. The light would be given to the Gentiles by the Israelites, not the other way around as it is today.

Now that we have made it clear that one cannot be saved through Christianity, and that Christ came for the children of Israel who are today the children of slavery, and only through the teachings of this doctrine by the chosen Israelite can the world; including Gentiles, be saved. Let us all now look at another angle; if salvation is of the Jews why look for it elsewhere? John 4:22.

The words of the Bible are often misinterpreted by so many different philosophies, and this is one of the reasons why some are going to great lengths to even change it from its original English form, to their own misinterpreted version. Some even gave God another name other than what the Bible says. Some are trying desperately to include themselves into the text. Others are trying to make it a universal book when it is not, for instance, in the Jehovah's Witness Book; Job is identified and portrayed as an oriental man. When I read this, I could not believe that I was actually seeing this nonsense in this Israelite book. It is very difficult for people to accept the fact that the Bible is an Israelite book, written by Israelites, about Israelites and for Israelites, case closed.

There are no orientals, or Gentiles, or any other people with God-given authority in that Bible. If a man is from the East in the United States, wouldn't that mean that he is from an eastern state? It wouldn't mean that he is from the east outside of the United States; then how come Job is the only Oriental among all the Israelites? Getting back to the subject matter of the spirit of Egypt among us. Maybe we never took the time to examine the way of life in this modern day Egypt, because if we look carefully, I am sure that we will be overwhelmed by the evidence of evil, injected into every aspect of our everyday lives. Let us take a closer look at some facts.

I will divide the year into two symbols. First the mountain which represents a time of light and life that God has chosen for Himself and His servants to serve Him; and to celebrate His Holy days. Our new world started from the mountain with Noah's ark. Moses had to climb the mountain to get instructions from God. Jesus had to climb the spiritual mountain to receive his power after being tempted by Satan. So the mountain remains symbolic to the Holiness of the most High God. On the other hand there is the valley or the pit, the lowest part of the earth. You will find an overflowing of substance that is very informative, and in keeping with the revealing of this spirit that lives among and around us, and in some cases within us. You will also find the unhidden facts, that were really meant to be hidden, amazing. We all know that Lucifer will be cast down into the bottomless pit. Hell is also identified with the pit. So now we have the mountain and the pit. How do we identify them, and how do we know them?

I am about to explore, and compare Biblically, that this new Egypt (America), is just like the old Egypt, and therefore is considered a strong representation of the pit. The following is a breakdown of time, proving the culture of America is based on the prophecy spoken by the prophets as is stated in Deut. 28.

The beginning of God's laws started in the time of Abib. This is the time when He brought his children out of Egypt, and this memory should have never been erased in the minds and hearts of the children of slavery and all those who believed that the God of Israel is their God. But the Christians removed the emphasis from this most Holy time to the coldest: January. The Khazarian's New Year is September-October. Their beginning is the end of God's Holy time. But ignorance is bliss.

If we count backwards from the seventh month of September,

March would be the first month of the year. This only makes sense because spring begins around March 21st, and the days get longer from then on. Flowers bloom in spring, the snow and ice begins to melt, the weather begins to warms up, etc. Obviously a new beginning.

The days from this point on are dominated with the increase of light. There are always twenty four hours in a day, but the light continues to dominate. The weather increases with warmth, the birds are singing, trees are budding and so on. On the fourteenth day of Abib (the first month), is the Passover (Feast of Unleavened Bread) for seven days.

Deut. 16:1 "Observe the month of Abib and keep the Passover unto the Lord thy God: For in the month of Abib the Lord thy God brought thee forth out of Egypt by night." Continue to read to Verse 8. Matthew 26:17 "Now the first day of the Feast of Unleavened Bread the disciples came to Jesus, saying unto him, where wilt thou that we prepare for thee to eat the Passover?" As it is clearly shown here, Jesus and His disciples kept the Passover.

Acts 20:6 "And we sailed away from Philippi after the <u>days of unleavened bread</u>, and came unto them to Troas in five days; where we abode seven days." This occurred after the death of Jesus and the resurrection of the Christ. Therefore proving that there is no difference between the Old Testament and the New. It all belongs to the Israelites. This also proves that the Israelites after the death of Jesus, still continued to keep the Passover. after the resurrection.

In a discussion that we had once, Elder Shadrock told us what he heard, and this is how he explained the confusion; **and I**

quote; "Is it true that some Israelites are now saying that we must not keep Passover in this land of our captivity? Because all the feasts of the Passover were kept in the land of Israel. I would like to challenge this statement as being false, rude and absurd. Number one; the land of Israel will never be our home again. Even though some children of slavery are still calling it their home today, it is nothing more than a cursed piece of real estate. Malachi 1: 3-5.

This scripture states clearly who will occupy the land in the last days, and who will throw it down and destroy it. It also states where God's words and doctrine will be magnified from, and it will be from the borders, or in other words, outside of that cursed land that we the children of Israel had defiled and now the children of Esau along with the children of Gog and Magog are continuously polluting. If you do not understand this scripture, how about reading Deuteronomy 28:68 over again and again until you do. Bearing in mind, it says that we will be brought into Egypt again with ships, and we shall see that land no more again.

Now when the children were in the land of Egypt, where was the first Passover kept? Was it kept in Israel? No it was not. We as a people are in Egypt again, brought here by ships. I would also like to ask, which is most important the history of our fathers, or the instructions from our God?

The history tells us that our fathers could not have kept the Passover in the land of their captivity then, because they were not allowed to; so everytime they went back from their captivity they kept it in their own land to give God praise. But since we are not going to see that land anymore, not ever again because of the disobedience of our fathers, should we then today disobey the instructions of our God? God forbid. Exodus 9-10.

The 11th. verse states that the God of Israel will give our fathers the land of Canaan. There is no law that says we should only keep the Passover in the land of Israel; none. But the law does say that we must keep it **from year to year**.

Now you tell me, which is most important? The history or the instructions? But then again, there are people who are in a hurry to change their names, to change the book, walking backwards contrary to the truth. In my opinion, teachers of the doctrine, because of spiritual blindness, cannot define the difference between what happened in the past (history) and what will happen in the future (prophecy). The instructions are very clear, and we must at all times carry them out - **unquote**.

Let me now get back to explaining the desertion of the mountain, and the overflowing and overcrowding of the pit in this Egypt. There are two periods in the year where we have equal amount of daylight and darkness. This occurs in the first month of Abib (March-April) and in the seventh month of Tishri (September-October). It is between these two periods that the foundation of the mountain is formed. This is the time when the statutes were given unto Israel. This time of the mountain was set aside for our God (a time most holy). The way to lay the foundation and to have a chance to climb the mountain, is by keeping the laws, statutes and commandments given to us (Israelites) from the God of Abraham, the God of Isaac and the God of Jacob. The way to the pit is simply to disobey.

We must celebrate our New Year on the New Moon closest to the Spring Equinox of March 21st. This is called the first Day of Abib. Abib is the first month in the Israelite calendar. At this time, the earth awakens and life begins to show itself. Exodus 12:1-2 & Exodus 13:1-4. Let us also try to study the story of Noah and the ark. Gen. 7:11-12 "In the six hundredth year of Noah's life, in the <u>second month</u>, the seventeenth day of the month, the same day were all the fountains of the great deep broken up, and the windows of heaven were opened. And the rain was upon the earth forty days and forty nights."

Gen. 7:18 "And the waters prevailed, and were increased greatly upon the earth; and the ark went upon the face of the waters." Read from Gen. 7:11-24. Here we read that the waters began to fall in the <u>second month</u> and <u>increased greatly</u>. Look at the graph, as the line ascends as the waters did.

Gen. 8:2-4 "The fountains also of the deep and the windows of heaven were stopped, and the rain from heaven was restrained. And the waters returned from off the earth continually: and after the end of the hundred and fifty days the waters were abated. And the ark <u>rested</u> in the <u>seventh month</u>, on the <u>seventeenth day of the month</u>, upon the mountain of Ararat." The graph outlines this completely, the waters increasing, then stopping and pulling back until the ark rests where? On the <u>mountains</u> of Ararat, on the <u>seventh month</u>, the <u>seventeenth day</u> of the month.

Genesis 8:5 "And the waters decreased continually until the <u>tenth month</u>: in the tenth month, on the first day of the month were the tops of the mountains seen." What is the lowest point on the graph? It is the tenth month (December), the waters decreased as the light also decreased and the darkness increased. Continue to read from Verse 6 on.

Gen. 8:13 "And it came to pass in the six hundredth and first year, in the <u>first month</u>, the <u>first day of the month</u>, the waters were dried up from off the earth: and Noah removed the covering of the ark, and looked, and behold, the face of the ground was dry." The ground was dry on the first day of Abib (Israelite New Year). Noah was now ready for the new beginning.

You will notice that the graph is forming a mountain where the beginning occurred with twelve hours of light and twelve hours of darkness. On the first day of Abib (Spring Equinox), climbing up to the peak in the fourth month, June 21st (Summer Solstice) and forming the other slope touching the twelve hours of darkness and twelve hours of light on September 23rd (Autumn Equinox). The Autumn Equinox is the seventh month known on the Israelite calendar as Tishri. This is also a very holy time for Israelites.

Once we pass through the seventh month, the line of the graph submerges below the 12/12 light. Now the darkness begins to dominate, as the world descends into the pit. These are the dark days recognized by the world.

Equinox: The time when the sun crosses the equator where day and night are of equal length all over the world.

September: comes from the Roman word "Septem" meaning Seven, or the seventh month. This is the end of the Holy period.

Let us now look at these dark days of the world, and the graph as it descends into the pit from the eighth month (October) to the twelveth month (February). The days of physical darkness and cold, frigid temperatures.

October: The eighth month of the primitive Roman year, which began in March. (Webster Dictionary).

November: The ninth month, according to the ancient Roman year. (Webster Dictionary). December: The tenth month of the Roman year.

The Roman calendar is referred to as primitive, but the New

Year change did not happen until quite recently. Until the year 1564 A.D., the New Year always started around March 25th. However, King Charles IX of France changed it to January 1st. The rest of Europe eventually followed suit. When you open your newspaper to your horoscope, the first astrological sign you see is Aires (March-April).

After reading in a dictionary, that this time was a Roman time, one will be inclined to believe that it all started in Rome. But this is only one way the Christians use to make themselves look good, by putting their own belief and interpretation in print. That is why we have so many versions of a single Bible.

We will discover that this time of what is known today as March-April was not originated in Rome, but existed even in the time when the children of Israel left Egypt.

In Italian the number 7 is "sette" (September), 8 is "otto" (October), 9 is "nove" (November) and 10 is "dieci" (December). The Italian language stems from the ancient Latin language. Today, the world celebrates New Year on January 1st, the coldest and also the darkest time of the year. How can a new beginning occur when the earth is frozen, dormant and asleep (dead)? Does it make any sense to you? The Christian celebrations of the pit, begins at the end of October, their first big event is "Halloween" on October 31st. This used to be, and still is the Satanic New Year. It is also known as "All Hallows" or "All Hallow Even." The use of the word "hallow", is a form of deception used by the disciples of the dark. Hallow meaning holy is being polluted for one to believe that celebrating the dead is holy, this is just another Christian lie. This is the time when in the satanic church, the high priest conducts the ritual mass of blood sacrifices.

This signals the end of summer leading to the winter cold, when the early Christians celebrated their winter carnival. It is also associated with the return of the dead to their homes, for ancestral worshipping, practiced in Europe by witches.

On November 1st "All Saint's Day" is also known as "All Hallow Day". These dark and unholy days, provide the Gentile pagans with the opportunity to really celebrate their pagan gods, which includes the lighting of candles to the dead, the commemorating of the martyrs in the Christian philosophy. It was officially instituted in 835 A.D. This form of worshipping the dead is ancestral worship dressed up in holy sheep clothing, but is really a wolf known as voodoo.

On November 2nd-3rd is the "Day of the Dead." Also known as "All Soul's Day." Mass is also kept when christians, satanists and pagans light candles to the dead and pray for them. The Catholic church has the requiem masses and memorial services.
On November 11th, "Remembrance Day" services and mass are kept on behalf of the <u>dead</u> soldiers killed in action. Gravesites are visited, with the placing of the wreath at the graves.

Do you see any difference with the above times from Halloween on? They are all dealing with the dead, in the dark times of the year, how appropriate. Is it a mere coincident when you visit the city of power; Washington, that you will find more than cemeteries? A place where the dead is honoured by carving of the dead bodies in stone statues, images of beasts and men, signs and symbols of the dead all over the place? One person told me about a year ago, that if you look carefully you will see Washington the seat of power, as nothing more than a city of the dead. If we go to the scriptures, we will also see how " the children of Israel" went wrong even from the eighth month.

Those who should know better and should not go by the way of the world. Read I Kings 12. The son of Solomon, Rehoboam, forsook the counsel of the elders and listened to the young men in Israel (Verse 8). Jeroboam and the other men returned unto him (Rehoboam) the third day. Rehoboam came down harder on them than his father Solomon. In Verse 16 you read how Israel departed all to their own tents. So Israel spilt up with the kingdom of Israel to the north and the kingdom of Judah to the south (Verse 19). Jeroboam was made king of Israel and Rehoboam continued to be king over Judah. You can also see how all of this had to happen (Verse 24), Israel would be rent after the days of Solomon. In Verse 28 we read how Jeroboam made two calves of gold, which is very familiar to the time when Israel came out of Egypt and Aaron did the same thing. He also made other men priests who weren't from the tribe of Levi. Now the clincher is Verses 32 & 33.

I Kings 12:32-33 "And Jeroboam ordained a feast in the eighth month, on the fifteenth day of the month, like unto the feast that is in Judah, and he offered upon the altar... So he offered upon the altar which he had made in Bethel the fifteenth day of the eighth month, even in the month <u>which he had devised of his own heart</u>; and ordained a feast unto the children of Israel: and he offered upon the altar, and burnt incense." So Israel was split and right away you can see the power of the lie. This man Jeroboam (an Israelite) did all things according to his <u>own heart</u>, not according to the instructions given unto the children of Israel by our God. It all took place during the <u>eighth month</u> (the same time as Halloween etc...), the time in which Israel was falling quickly into the "pit." The physical darkness dominated, and the spiritual took control.

As we continue on the graph, there is the American Thanksgiving, kept on the last Thursday of November as instituted by President Lincoln in 1864. It is in essence a national harvest celebration and was first observed by the pilgrim fathers at Plymouth in 1621. Harvest at the end of November? The season is a little too cold for harvesting. Don't you think?

On December 21st is the Winter Solstice (in the tenth month), which is the darkest day of the year. In southern Ontario there is a total of fifteen hours of darkness plus a few minutes on that day, leaving roughly nine hours of light. This is the same day that the high priest performs his ritual mass of blood sacrifices. This is leading us right to the pagan Christmas. Remember all of this happens during the darkest time of the year. For those who have eyes to see, let them see. Christianity would keep its midnight mass on Christmas Eve. Catholics in particular, others just observe it as a culture.

From the 26th day of December, for one week is kept the time of "Kwansa." A time of harvest. Harvest what? In the snow of December. This is just another black Christmas, given to a people in need of identity, and know not where to find it. Which leads us of course to January 1st (New Year). A new beginning in the coldest time of the year. Does this make sense? January used to be the 11th month. What happened? This leads us to January 6th, when the Eastern Orthodox church (Christian) celebrates the birth of their jesus. What's going on? How many birthdays could one Jesus have anyway? A better question would be, how many "jesuses" are there?

The Israelite Jesus, was born in the seventh month of Tishri. The time of light and the mountain. Not in the time of darkness and the pit. But the lie is strong and the multitudes are increasing rapidly. Israel was always the smallest of all nations and it is no different in this day.

The tenth month is the lowest point of the pit. Let's examine what happened to the Israelites during the same month. Let's go to the scriptures beginning with the book of Ezra, which touches on the ninth month first. Read Ezra 10:1-17.

In Verse 16, we read how they sat down to examine the matter on the <u>first day</u> of the <u>tenth month</u>. In other words, Israel began to clean house and start from fresh hoping that the God of Israel would return to them. Verse 17 "...and they made an end with all the men that had taken strange wives by the <u>first day of the first month</u>." The first day of the first month (look at the graph), so Israel could start new at the beginning of the New Year, with the God of Israel as the foundation. The mountain would again ascend with the light (truth) dominating the picture.

Ezekiel 24:1 "Again in the ninth year, in the tenth month, in the tenth day of the month, the word of the Lord came unto me, saying..." Here we can see how the tenth month is emphasized to Ezekiel (the prophet), while Israel is in captivity in Babylon.

Verse 2, "Son of man, write thee the name of the day, even this same day: the king of Babylon set himself against Jerusalem this same day." The lesson to be gained is that Israelites should learn from their past mistakes so that they strive not to repeat them today nor in the future. The House of Israel is a disobedient nation unto their God, but luckily our God doesn't change. He is the same yesterday, today and tomorrow.

Ecc. 1:9 "The thing that hath been, it is that which shall be; and that which is done is that which shall be done: and there is no new thing under the sun." The tenth month (refer to the graph), again the lowest point in the pit.

Ezekiel 33:21 "And it came to pass in the twelfth year of our captivity in the tenth month, in the fifth day of the month, that one that had escaped out of Jerusalem came unto me, saying, the city is smitten." Continue to read until Verse 29 and you'll see how Israel is continued to be punished, for they broke the first and most important commandment. "Hear Oh Israel, The Lord our God, the Lord is One."

Let's go back to the world events during the time of the pit. In February there is "carnival" in the West Indies and parts of the Americas. Valentine's Day on February 14th, a time of so-called love. Is there any saint in the Bible by the name of Valentine? *See "All you need to know about Saints" pg.55 The Forgotten Israelites by Shadrock.* Then there is what the Catholics call "Lent", forty days leading to what they call "Palm Sunday", which is seven days before Easter, originally a pagan feast of a wild sexual nature. Note how the lie has taken so much from the Israelites and used it for their own pagan purpose.

Revelation 14:1 "And I looked, and, lo, a Lamb stood on the Mount Sion, and with him an hundred and forty and four thousand, having his Father's name written in their foreheads." Read Verse 5. Also Revelation 17, highlighting Verses 8 & 9.

Revelation 17:8 "The beast that thou sawest was, and is not: and shall ascend out of the bottomless pit, and go into perdition: and they that dwell on the earth shall wonder, whose names were not written in the book of life from the foundation of the world, when they behold the beast that was, and is not, and yet is. And here is the mind which hath wisdom. The seven heads are seven <u>mountains</u>, on which the woman sitteth." Revelation 17 deals with the "Great Whore", which is Christianity. All those times kept during the dark period (the pit on the graph) are based on the Christian philosophy. "...and shall ascend out of the bottomless pit." Her ambition is to get on that mountain, and the day this happens, it will most certainly be the end.

Revelation 21:10 "And he carried me away in the spirit to a great and high mountain, and shewed me that great city, the holy Jerusalem, descending out of heaven from God." This is clearly spiritual, a "New Jerusalem".

After examining carefully all the facts, you can see where the system itself is deep-rooted in the ways of Lucifer. You should be able to see Christianity as the trail blaster of the Great Whore. You must be able to see the truth, and make your choice;

"The Mountain or the Pit ?".

THE TREE IN EGYPT

It is so interesting to sit back and take note of what a Christmas tree means to a christian home, how it has been said that the tree becomes the centre point of the home and brings the family closer together. When I hear statements like this, I can't help but to see no difference between voodoo and Christianity. By the way there is <u>no</u> difference. In the voodoo temple all the participants gather together around the centre pole and dance allowing "the spirit" to take hold and manifest itself. The pole is a tree stump and works as an altar. The christians gather around their tree, singing songs and every time they go to place a gift under the tree they pay homage to it by bowing or kneeling to reach under. By reaching under, they are also extending their hands to the tree. They are worshipping the tree. This might appear like a <u>very</u> innocent act to the blind, but we should be able to recognize the deception and be totally aware of what's going on.

CONIFEROUS COMPARED TO DECIDUOUS

The coniferous tree does not bear fruit that is eatable. We also know that it doesn't shed its needles (leaves) annually. It is forever awake no matter what season we are in. One can look at the tree in winter or summer or fall or even spring and it basically has the same appearance. It is very deceptive on the outside. Basically you can say it is like the dead. It is one way and one way only. You can't recognize signs by looking at it.

On the other side of the coin the deciduous tree shows a lot of movement throughout the year. In the spring it begins to bud and the leaves begin to grow. If it is a fruit tree, it also grows flowers which are the beginning stage of the fruit.

What this picture is saying is that one can recognize the times by just looking at the tree and taking a picture. Take a picture in the middle of each of the four seasons and compare them. You'll be able to see much in each of the four pictures. Try it.

When you look at a cedar (coniferous tree), it is forever green. You don't know what it is about, it is always the same in appearance (very deceiving).

At Christmas the evergreen tree would be decked with silver and gold, then the Christians sing their song for the season of the dead called, "Silver and Gold." How much plainer can it be? In Jeremiah 10 Verse 8, those that base their lives on what this tree represents, refers to "the stock is a doctrine of vanities." The silver would come from Tyre (Tarshish) which is in Lebanon, and the gold from Uphaz in Arabia (Ethiopia) working together from the hands <u>of the founder</u>. Their clothing is of blue and purple, two colours of Israel. Those that are aware seek to have power like the Israelites, for they have heard of the power of the God of Israel. Let me ask, was not Lucifer there and knows even the secrets but to give the breath of life? Whenever the Israelites were prospering being obedient to their God, they did have plenty of gold and silver. Beware of the tree. The tree in the garden was Lucifer. The tree cast down in Lebanon yesterday was the same man, and so is the tree in Egypt today; and in the day we partake of that tree, there will be no gold nor silver, no hope, no salvation for the children of God. Let us turn to Jeremiah 10:1-8.

Jeremiah 10:3-5 "For the custom of the people are vain: for one cutteth a tree out of the forest, the work of the hands of the workman, with the axe. They deck with silver and with gold; they fasten it with nails and with hammers, that it move not. They are upright as the palm tree but speak not: they must needs be borne, because they cannot go. Be not afraid of them: for they cannot do evil, neither also is it in them to do good."

Does this sound familiar? The key is that this practise of tree worship has been going on for a very long time. Let me remind you this was way before the birth of Jesus. Now let's go back to the same chapter 10 and bring out Verses 1 & 2.

Jeremiah 10:1-2 "Hear ye the word which the Lord speaketh unto you. <u>O House of Israel</u>. Thus saith the Lord, <u>Learn not the way of the heathen</u>, and be not dismayed at the signs of heaven; for the heathen are dismayed at them."

The God of Israel is <u>clearly</u> warning His children <u>not to do as the heathen</u>. So let me ask you, who are these people who put up evergreen trees? Are they not Christians? So it is very clear to see for those who have eyes that Christianity is not of the God spoken about in the Bible. You can also read more about the separation between an Israelite and a heathen in the book of Matthew 18:15-17. Do we then all worship the same God? It is important to note that from the book of Genesis to the book of Revelation, the God of Israel <u>only</u> speaks to His children and no one else.

So who is behind this cleverly, schemed deception? Who controls the world? Genesis 2:16-17 "And the Lord God commanded the man, saying, of every tree of the garden thou mayest freely eat. But of the tree of the knowledge of good and evil, thou shalt not eat of it: for in the day that thou eatest thereof thou shalt surely die." God clearly warned Adam and Eve of this man that stood out amongst God's host, not to deal with him. He being in the midst of the garden (the heavenly host). Let us now go to the book of <u>Ezekiel</u> and read about his wisdom and beauty that Eve could not resist. Read Ezekiel 31:3-9.

Ezekiel 28:2 "... I am God, I sit in the seat of God, in the midst of the seas; yet thou art a man, and not God..." You can see here how Lucifer wants to be God but cannot be for he is but a man. The power and might that he holds is shown by the way that he thinks. Read the following verses.

Ezekiel 28:3-4 "Behold, thou art wiser than Daniel; there is no secret that they can hide from thee. With thy wisdom and with thine understanding thou hast gotten thee riches, and hast gotten gold and silver into thy treasures:" We are seeing here a lot of power. Continue to read the chapter verse by verse. Read how Lucifer is described in Verses 12-14. Also explained is that he was described as the "anointed cherub." He would be removed from the mountain of God, being cast down. (Verses 16 & 17). Cast down with all that power that he possesses.

Ezekiel 31:3 "Behold, the Assyrian was a cedar in Lebanon with fair branches, and with a shadowing shroud, and of an high stature ; and his top was among the thick boughs."
Ezekiel 31:15-16 "Thus saith the Lord God; in the day that he went down into the grave I caused a mourning: I covered the deep for him, and I restrained the floods thereof, and the great waters were stayed: AND I CAUSED LEBANON TO MOURN FOR HIM, and all the trees of the field fainted for him. I made the nations to shake at the sound of his fall, when I cast him down to hell with them that descend into pit: and all the trees of Eden, the choice and best of Lebanon, all that drink water, shall be comforted in the nether parts of the earth." Lebanon, a land of war and destruction. A land that recently has never experienced peace. Whenever you even hear a bit of news about Lebanon on T.V. or radio, unto this day is bombing, killing and massacre.

These actions will eventually spread whenever the time is right for Lucifer to manifest in the land of Egypt. It is the duty or mandate of Lucifer to destroy any and everything of God that include God's children; " the children of slavery". What makes anyone think that a General would not seek to destroy his enemy's property, and his stock, and his house-hold. This is a logical principle of war, and there will be war in heaven and in earth in that day.

Lucifer's resting place was Lebanon, but as the time draweth near for the battle; when the four hundred years of God's children in this new Egypt comes to a close. Be not surprised, that the preparation time is also coming to a close, and he is now preparing for an all out war on the children of slaves. For when God's children are destroyed, who then will be his true representative on this earth? The signs of that war are being felt even today. The children of slavery are at their lowest point; while God is striking with natural disasters like never before in Asia, Europe, and America.

The world should stop looking to the land Israel for any signs of God, for there is nothing there to look forward to, but death and destruction.
The real children of Israel are no longer in the land of Canaan, or Palestine.
Note carefully, that the land was named after the children in their time (Israel). Which before was known as Canaan. When they were removed by enslavement, the land was called Palestine.
Note the reverse today. The occupants are again calling the land Israel, but are naming themselves after the land; "Israelis."
God had thrown down Lucifer next door to the land that he had given to his children, also next door to the old Egypt. Now if

his children are no longer there, but instead were shipped in ships to the New Egypt, where do you think Satan would be? Remember what the scriptures says; how powerful was this tree. The other trees in the Garden was not like him.

Ezekiel 31:8-9 "The cedars in the garden of God could not hide him; the fir trees were not like his boughs, and the chestnut trees were not like his branches; not any tree in the garden of God was like unto him in his beauty. I have made him fair by the multitude of his branches: so that all the trees of Eden, that were in the Garden of Eden, that were in the Garden of God, envied him."

After reading and understanding this scripture, why would anyone not only put a so-called Christmas tree in their home, but why would the Christian church endorse and encourage it, even decorate their church lawn with this tree? If you do not believe me, take a trip to Washington D.C., the capital of Egypt, and travel along 16th Street and you will discover so many different houses of various philosophies (churches), most with their lovely innocent looking evergreen trees on their front lawns, or at the entrance to their place of worship..

Actually you can read all of Ezekiel chapter 31. Later I will emphasize some other verses from this chapter but for now let's go to Ezekiel 28:1-4.

The national emblem of Lebanon is the tree (cedar of Lebanon). A tree that is known for its fragrance and durable wood. The resin from the trunk of the tree was also used in the embalming of the dead. The trees are found at altitudes of about 6,500 feet. The flowers open in September or October, which is peculiar to the cedars. Take note of the time: the end of God's, and the beginning of Lucifer's. The cones are 7-10 cm. in length, initially violet - purple turning to a dark green - grey. The cones are born upright on the top side of the branches. These trees are known to grow to heights of 400 feet. One foot for each year of the slavery of Israelites (Gen. 15:13 - 400 years). One foot has also 12 inches which relates to 12 months in a year, but most important of all, it relates to the 12 tribes of Israel, whom Lucifer must suppress and oppress and weaken, for these are those chosen by his enemy; God. Wow, just take a look at the picture and see the truth.

In this modern Egypt, a father would get up early in the morning on a cold winter day and go out with the family into the forest for a Christmas tree. They'd all agree on the same one, Dad would cut it with an axe to the ground and drag it all the way home. Once they are home they try to bring it back to life (Jeremiah 10). Nailing it to two sticks making a cross at the base and standing it up. Decorate the tree with silver and gold (Ezekiel 28:4 & Jeremiah 10:4), putting lights on it (formerly candles). Everyone has got to at least put one ornament on it (tradition) and last but not least a star is placed on the top of the tree. Water is then given to the tree so that the needles do not dry too quickly and fall off.

Is man playing God here? Trying to resurrect something that is dead. The roots of the tree no longer exist. The life of the tree is removed. Man is going through the motions of the "casting down" process. He is now trying to give the "breath of life" to this stump. The tree will just wither away and die, the root has been removed from long ago.

The star placed at the top of the tree representing the heavens, that light. But this is a light corrupted, let's read Amos 5:26. "But ye have borne the tabernacle of your Moloch and Chiun your images, the star of your god, which ye made to yourselves." Read also II Corinthians 11:14 " And no marvel; for Satan himself is transformed into an angel of light."

The shape of the tree is also the shape of the pyramid. The pyramid represents death, for it was a tomb unto the Egyptians where many were buried. How appropriate for the tree to look this way. When one prays as the Christians do, they clasp their hands again forming the appearance of the evergreen tree. Let's read some scriptures on the cedars of Lebanon.
Psalm 29:5&6 "The voice of the Lord breaketh the cedars: yea, the Lord breaketh the cedars to Lebanon. He maketh them also to skip like a calf: Lebanon and Sirion like a young unicorn." The God of Israel makes it very clear with what's going to happen to these strong and very durable trees (physical & spiritual).

The height of the cedar in Lebanon is truly incredible. It reaches so high up that one would get dizzy looking towards the top of it. In the scriptures we read how the enemy of Israel is compared like unto the cedar in stature. It would take the hand of the God of Israel to destroy this very powerful and capable enemy.
Amos 2:9 "Yet destroyed I the Amorite before them, whose height was like the height of the cedars, and he was strong as the oaks; yet I destroyed his fruit from above and his roots from beneath." In the Garden of Eden Lucifer rose above and stood out from among all the others that were there (the host of God). He was so daring and so clever in his ways that Eve couldn't resist

him. He is just as powerful, deceptive, full of knowledge, wise, etc. in every way <u>today</u> as <u>yesterday</u>. We must now note the time spoken of in Deut. 28:68; and what this tree got to do with it? Well in the very same year when America was given her role as the new Egypt, the strength and symbol of Lucifer was also transported to her shores.

The very first ever Christmas tree came to the so-called New World through America in 1776 by Hessian soldiers during the American Revolution. Later on the German immigrants brought it with them, and another page of the prophecy is fulfilled. This individual custom could have died like so many before or after, but if it did, the scriptures would not have been fulfilled. That is why the tree did not remain only in the homes of those German immigrants; but became a national celebration and worship.

In the early 1900s important places of power would put up the largest of these trees, places like Rockefeller Plaza in New York, and of course in the White House. Now no tree in the garden of the world is like unto her, she is towering over every other tree, and her roots are by great waters. She is at the centre of the world in power and influence.

But before I close let me read Revelation.13:9-10 " If any man have an hear let him hear. He that leadeth into captivity, shall go into captivity: He that killeth with the sword, must be killed with the sword. Here is the patience and the faith of the saints".

May the Children of Slavery take heed. May them that sojourn with the Children of Slavery take heed. May all those who sincerely believe that the children of slavery are the true Children of Israel take heed. May all the Israelite Saints take heed. May all the Household of the Children of Israel take heed.

RETAIL PRICE LIST
Books you must read.
By SHADROCK

(1) THE TRUTH THE LIE AND THE BIBLE

(2) THE FORGOTTEN ISRAELITES
God's Chosen People

(3) THE WORD THE ISRAELITES AND THE DAMNED

(4) THE SPIRIT OF EGYPT IN AMERICA
By Michael Hinds

NAME_____

ADDRESS_____

_____

_____

PHONE (_____)_____

Send me _____ (copies) of # 1
Send me _____ (copies) of # 2
Send me _____ (copies) of # 3
Send me _____ (copies) of # 4

Any book $13.95 @.
Send money order to:

FIFTH RIBB PUBLISHING,
P.O. BOX 287, STATION E.
TORONTO, ONTARIO
CANADA M6H-4E2

www.ingramcontent.com/pod-product-compliance
Lightning Source LLC
Chambersburg PA
CBHW050555300426
44112CB00013B/1934